SQUASH

SQUASH

JOHN TAYLOR

PELHAM BOOKS
Stephen Greene Press

For my parents

PELHAM BOOKS/Stephen Greene Press

Published by the Penguin Group
27 Wrights Lane, London w8 5tz, England
Viking Penguin Inc., 40 West 23rd Street, New York, New York 10010, USA
The Stephen Greene Press, Inc., 15 Muzzey Street, Lexington,
Massachusetts 02173, USA
Penguin Books Australia Ltd, Ringwood, Victoria, Australia
Penguin Books Canada Ltd, 2801 John Street, Markham, Ontario, Canada l3r 1b4
Penguin Books (NZ) Ltd, 182–190 Wairau Road, Auckland 10, New Zealand

Penguin Books Ltd, Registered Offices: Harmondsworth, Middlesex, England

First published 1985
Paperback edition 1987
Revised paperback edition 1989
Copyright © John K. Taylor, 1985 and 1989

Made and printed in Great Britain by
Butler & Tanner Ltd, Frome and London

A CIP catalogue record for this book is available from the British Library.

isbn 0 7207 1879 1

Unless otherwise credited all photographs are by Steve Powell, Allsport.
Line drawings by Edwina Keene.

Contents

Foreword by Jonah Barrington, MBE   7

Acknowledgements   8

Introduction   9

1 The strokes   11

2 Playing the game   51

3 Tournament preparation and play   75

4 Fitness training   85

5 Practice: the way to perfect your game   121

6 The mental approach – it's all in the mind   132

Appendix I: The rules of the international singles game of
squash rackets   139

Appendix I.I: Definitions   152

Appendix II: Dimensions of a singles court   155

Appendix III: Specification of a racket   156

Appendix IV: Specification for squash-racket balls   157

Appendix V: Colour of players' clothing   157

Appendix VI: Code of conduct   158

Index   159

Foreword

by Jonah Barrington, MBE

John Taylor has written the most modern instructional book on the game of squash. This does not surprise me in the least as I must confess that after closely linking with him at National Junior Squad level I would have expected only the best from his mind and pen. Moreover I am delighted that he should have decided to go into print as there have been in recent years too many misleading manuals foisted on the unsuspecting squash public.

John is meticulously accurate in his breakdown of the fundamental strokes and the technical aspect of squash and yet he makes the reader continually aware that, whereas there are good traditional guidelines, these are not the last words on the game. He suggests, and rightly so, that there are many, many ways of hitting a squash ball well and accordingly players of the very highest calibre frequently construct the same marvellous strokes quite differently. How tedious it would be if everybody played the same way!

I especially like John's attitude to the fitness and training aspects of the sport. He is as convinced as I am that only hard work evinces results but it must be done with great care and attention to detail. Both John and I have gleaned much from the professional advisory services of the physiotherapist Vivian Grisogono and exercise physiologist Dr Craig Sharp, and their outstanding expertise is clearly manifest in the text of this most excellent book.

Above all we are provided with an encyclopaedia of accurate information for all levels of play – from the beginners through to those with world championship ambitions. Just to add, as it were, a touch of spice John has ensured the very best of illustrations liberally spread throughout a book which I have much enjoyed and most heartily recommend.

Jonah Barrington

Acknowledgements

Many people have helped directly and indirectly with the writing of this book. Particularly, a special word of thanks to Jonah Barrington for agreeing to write the foreword and allowing me to use his photograph on the front cover. Also for sharing his love and knowledge of the game while I worked with him with the National Junior Squads and the England Under-19 team. Other coaches, too, at squad weekends contributed ideas to this book, none more so than Graham Stevenson.

Thanks especially to Vivian Grisogono, sports physiotherapist, and Dr Craig Sharp, Co-director of the Human Motor Performance Laboratory (University of Birmingham), as the chapters on fitness and training could not have been written without their assistance. Both have worked with the National Junior Squads and freely shared their vast knowledge and generously gave their time to help me.

Any sports coaching book relies on its photographs to illustrate the text. Steve Powell, of All-Sport, patiently helped to shoot the technique sequences while Stephen Line and Robin Ely Jones contributed the match-play photographs. Thanks for giving their time must go to Jane Reeves, David Pearson, Andy Dwyer, Jamie Hickox, Bob Johnson and Andrew Sceats who acted as willing models for both the photographs and the line illustrations, the latter skilfully produced by Edwina Keene. Also to the Arena Club in London for allowing me to use their facilities for a photographic session. I am grateful to the Squash Rackets Association for their co-operation in providing a copy of the up-to-date ISRF rules of the singles game of squash. Thanks also go to Sara Huntingdon for her comments based on her experience with the 'Inner Game' in this country, which helped in preparing the chapter on mental preparation.

Finally, grateful thanks to both Lesley Gowers and Bob Eames who patiently guided me throughout the writing of this book; I hope it was not too much of a trial for them.

JOHN TAYLOR
April, 1985

Introduction

The prime aim of this book is to arm the ambitious squash player with the knowledge to fulfil his or her potential and to achieve his or her own individual goal in the sport. As you read it, I hope it will stimulate you to work at your game. The book deals in some detail with the five areas in which a squash player must reach a high standard to be successful: he must be physically fit, in good health, have the correct mental approach and be technically and tactically sound.

In squash there is not just one way to hit a ball: you have only to watch the top players in the world to realize that. However, it is important to develop a good basic technique from which to evolve your own style. This book covers the whole spectrum of hitting a squash ball, from the basics to more advanced stroke variations, to help you build up your shot vocabulary.

There is a chapter on how to practise, outlining specific practices for all the shots discussed in the section on stroke variations. The old saying that 'practice makes perfect' is as true today as when it was first uttered. Any improvement will only be achieved through hard work: there is no easy way.

Squash has often been likened to chess. It is very much a 'cat-and-mouse' game, each player trying to out-think the other. The tactical side is examined in detail from elementary to advanced match tactics.

You need to get fit to play squash, not play squash to get fit. The chapter on training looks into the physiological background of fitness and considers the different aspects of fitness required for squash. Training, to be effective, must be individually tailored to a player's strengths and weaknesses: there is a section outlining how to plan your own training schedule safely to improve your fitness, also going into detail about stretching and body management.

Mental preparation is an often-neglected aspect of squash. Many a match has been lost in the mind before the player steps on to court, because he has become too nervous or is not keyed-up for the match ahead. The final chapter explores ways of coping with nerves, so that you arrive on court mentally prepared for your match.

Chapter by chapter, I hope you find the information to help you become a better squash player. This is not something anyone else can do for you – you must have the heart and will and the 'bottle' for the hard work ahead, if you are to achieve your goal. The higher your ambition, the more dedicated you must be.

Author's note

For the sake of simplicity, throughout the text I have used 'he', 'him', etc., when referring to players. However, the book is aimed at men and women players alike and I hope female readers will not feel slighted.

The strokes

It is very important to master the basic forehand swing and backhand swing in squash, as all other shots in the game originate from these two. For this reason, it is essential to look at the basic swing in detail. Once a skill is clearly understood, learning follows much more easily.

The anatomy of the swing starts with the grip.

The grip

The 'continental' or 'shake hands' grip. The 'V' formed between the thumb and the first finger pointing along the forehand edge of the shaft gives an open racket face. INSET: *Note the first finger curled around the handle to aid racket head control, with the three other fingers evenly spread.*

This is the same for both the forehand and backhand strokes: in squash there is not enough time to change the grip when altering your stroke as there is in tennis. Some variation in grip is bound to occur among the top professionals, of course, which is the case in most sports, but by and large the essential features of a good grip are as described in the following paragraphs.

The grip used in squash is known as the 'continental' or 'shake hands' grip. You should master it correctly in order to attain consistent stroke production. To achieve this grip, hold the racket by the shaft in your left hand* with its head vertical, then 'shake hands' with the handle with your right hand. There should be a 'V' between your thumb and index finger, which points along the forehand (left) edge of the shaft of the racket as you look down on to the top

* The text assumes that players are right-handed.

of the racket. The heel of your hand should be about an inch from the butt and your index finger curled around the handle, as this will aid racket-head control. The three remaining fingers are curled round the handle, with the thumb resting on the second finger.

The grip in squash must be firm enough to prevent the racket flying out of the hand, but sufficiently relaxed not to cause tension in the forearm, hindering good stroke production. Initially you may find this grip difficult to master and also that it changes during a rally. Persevere, however: keep checking your grip in between rallies, using the 'V' between the thumb and index finger as a guide.

The swing   The racket should be an extension of your arm so that both it and your body are working in harmony, not fighting against each other. A relaxed rhythm to the swing is essential.

There are many elements that go together to make up the basic swing: good footwork, balance, preparation, downswing, open racket face on impact, weight transference and follow-through. Think of the 'four Bs' when working on grooving your swing: bat, body, ball and brain.

In squash, the wrist plays a very important part in the swing. A cocked wrist is essential to a good swing, not just in the preparation but throughout the stroke. Keep the racket head up – not drooping down by your ankles – when striking the ball. Squash is often referred to as a 'wristy' game, but this does not mean that you should play with a 'floppy' wrist.

Remember, too, that early preparation is essential in this game, so that you have time to play a controlled shot, though obviously

there will be occasions when stroke production is rushed.

The swing can be likened to a throwing action when skimming a stone across water. Draw the arm back as though you were going to do this – though instead of a stone in your hand, you have a racket, with your wrist cocked. This means that the head of your racket is near your right ear for the forehand (left ear for the backhand) and your arm is bent at the elbow. The elbow should be a comfortable distance away from the body so that you are not cramped, as this stops a free downswing. In preparation, the racket head should be taken back first, followed by the wrist and lastly the elbow. The preparation of the racket does not have to be high for an effective stroke, but it is important that the racket is taken back straight. This helps the racket head to come down to hit through the ball rather than across the body.

The sequence on the downswing is the exact opposite: elbow, wrist and lastly the racket head. At impact, the wrist and racket head are level, with the face of the racket slightly open. For the forehand, the impact is level with the leading foot, and just in front of it for the backhand. (This applies to straight drives.) If the ball is to go where you want at impact, the open racket face must point in the direction you are aiming and then on the follow-through continue in that direction. The arm should be straight at impact, so you are stroking the ball at a comfortable distance from the body.

Follow through the ball, then as the racket head points towards the front wall, the elbow should once again bend, so that the follow-through continues safely up. This means a safe swing which does not endanger your opponent by swinging across your body.

The swing is a circular one, with the arm bent in the preparation phase, straight at impact and bent again on the follow-through.

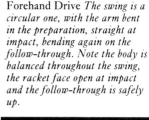

Forehand Drive *The swing is a circular one, with the arm bent in the preparation, straight at impact, bending again on the follow-through. Note the body is balanced throughout the swing, the racket face open at impact and the follow-through is safely up.*

Backhand Drive *The swing for the backhand is also circular like that of the forehand. Impact, though, is further forward with the racket face open. The body is balanced throughout, following through safely with the racket up.*

Racket-head speed through the hitting area is important to generate power to the shot. However, a relaxed rhythm to your swing is essential: any snatching only detracts from the end result. Think of a smooth swing as you perform the action and do not try to strike the ball too hard.

Generally speaking, when there is time, correct footwork will aid stroke production. When you are under pressure, it is often necessary to improvise because of the speed of squash. The forehand side of the court is the area where most players tend to play off the wrong foot; on the backhand, however, generally players are more correct.

Good footwork aids balance, which is essential in squash. Try to arrive in good time to play the ball, stepping across with the left foot for a forehand and the right foot for a backhand. The leading leg should be bent, so that on the downswing the weight is transferred on to the leading foot. The timing of the shot is greatly helped by this: it will enable you to lean into the ball on impact. When playing the ball off the wrong foot, a player's body weight is generally not transferred into the shot, so accuracy and power are lost. Wherever possible, try to ensure that you are always transferring your weight into the shot to help generate pace.

Every player has an optimum distance from the ball that is comfortable; when striking the ball, try to achieve a balanced stance, neither over-reaching, nor too upright – both hinder good stroke production. The two areas of your body that should bend when you are playing a shot are your back and knees.

To help you picture what to do when stepping across your body, imagine a clock face. For the forehand, aim for two o'clock; and for the backhand, nine o'clock. This helps to ensure that you step

across, not forward, when playing the ball and is especially important when playing from the front third of the court.

Develop good habits with your footwork and don't become lazy – this only leads to mistakes which cost points. Ask yourself constantly: 'Am I in a balanced position?' Poor footwork on the forehand often means that the player is open-chested, so losing accuracy, dragging the ball away from the side wall or continually playing across court from the front.

In the squash swing, the head plays an important role: move the head and the shoulders rotate. The effect is loss of accuracy, especially when attempting to hit straight. Try to discipline yourself and keep your head still, eye on the ball, till after impact and you will find that this helps you to be more accurate. Jonny Leslie, the winner of the last British Amateur Championship in 1979, keeps his head still longer than necessary when knocking up, to discipline himself to groove his swing, so that when the match starts there is no unnecessary movement of the head and shoulders.

In summary, prepare early, step into the ball so that your body is sideways to it, have a relaxed, smooth swing with the impact at a comfortable distance from the body and opposite the leading foot for the forehand and just in front of it for the backhand, striking the ball where possible at the top of its bounce with an open racket face, transferring your weight into the shot and finally remember to follow through up. Your opponents will appreciate this.

Remember: a sound, grooved, basic swing will help you to master all shots in squash. Try to understand the swing so that if something is going wrong during a match, you can put it right. Practice makes perfect, but more of that later in the book. You are now ready to move on to the basic shots played in squash.

Service

As one can only score points when serving, it is therefore important that great care is taken with the service. The professionals appear not to take much care over this aspect of the game, but this is far from the truth. Watch Jonah Barrington serve, for example: he attempts, every time, to exert maximum pressure on his opponent. It is the one free shot in the game, so make the most of it.

A good service is worth 3 or 4 points a game – not necessarily aceing your opponent, but because it puts him on the defensive and you in the driving seat on the 'T' in control of the rally. A weak service gives your opponent the chance of attacking, so taking away the initiative from you.

Service is the one shot in the game when you don't have to run for the ball, so take full advantage of this. Look at the position you are in on the court and where your opponent is standing. You are level with the 'T', he is standing behind the service box – in other words, behind you, so let's keep him there with you in command of the court. Now consider how your service can help you maintain your positional superiority.

Firstly, where should the ball go? Ideally it should travel after the front wall on to the side wall, approximately level with the back of the service box, and then bounce on to the floor, ideally dying in the back corner. If you aim the ball to strike the side wall, this puts doubts in your opponent's mind about volleying the return of service. If he lets the ball bounce into the back corner, he is forced on to the defensive, having to play the ball out of the back corner and probably setting you up with a weak reply, thus giving you the opportunity to dominate the rally.

Service *From the right box. Note the stance in the service box. From this position the body naturally moves across easily to the 'T'.*

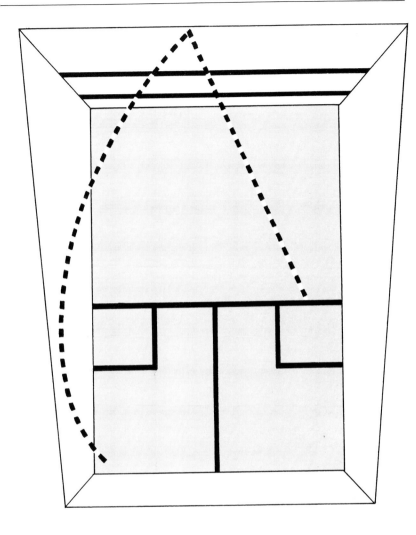

Flight path of the ball for the lob service from the right service box.

'T' position Having served, move smartly across to the 'T', racket up, watching your opponent and ready to move quickly.

Second, how do you achieve this devastating service? I have already stated that you don't have to run to return the ball, so consider, to begin with, the service box. The secret of success of any shot is consistency, and this is easier to achieve with the serve. First, position your feet in the service box. It is important to adopt the same stance for every serve: I suggest the right foot in the box (not touching the line – remember that this is a foot fault) and the left outside the box (see photograph), standing about a foot back from the front of the right service box. This position gives you an easy path across to just behind the 'T'. When serving from the left,

Flight path of the ball for the lob service from the left service box.

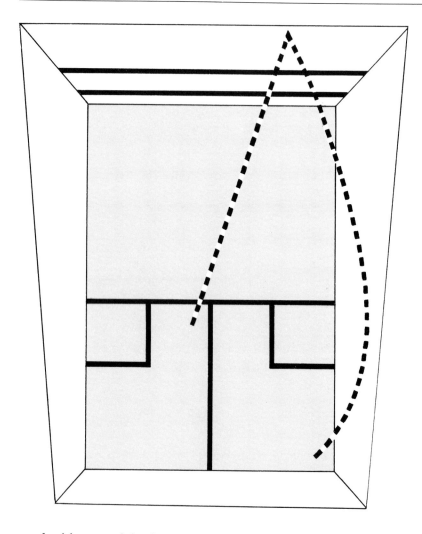

stand with your right foot in the service box and step out across towards the centre of the court as you strike the ball.

Having taken up your position in the service box, pick your spot on the front wall, where you are aiming the ball to strike. When you are serving from the right box, this is just left of centre; when you are serving from the left box, it is two thirds of the way across the front wall. These target areas (see line illustration) will help you to achieve width to your serve, a very important element to successful serving.

Opposite: Lob Serve The lob serve demonstrated from the left-hand box. Note the position of the feet in the service box, the open racket face on impact giving the ball height, and the follow-through up.

After picturing the spot on the front wall for which you are aiming, check where your opponent is standing. Do not take it for granted that he is standing just behind the back of the service box; he may have taken up a forward position to try to attack your serve.

This short checklist – position of feet, spot on the front wall and noting the position of the receiver – will have the effect of making you take time, and so care, over your service. Despite what many club and above-standard players say, the serve is a very valuable weapon, so don't waste it. Like any other shot in squash, your service requires practice to perfect it.

When practising the serve on your own, experiment until you have a picture in your mind of where you have to hit the front wall to achieve the desired result: time spent will not be wasted. Make your service an asset to your game, not a liability. Remember: you are in the driving seat and your opponent is on the receiving end, so make life as awkward as possible for him.

The guidelines I have given will help with the lob, driven and hard serves, as long as you are aiming to strike the side wall. If you are trying to serve at your opponent, or down the middle, the target on the front wall is different.

Now let's look in detail at the different service variations.

A much underrated serve in squash is the lob, which many players **Lob serve** of club standard and above find difficult to return. It is well worth perfecting. Imagine a high, floating ball with no pace on it, angled in towards the side wall: volley it and there is a risk of a miss-hit, especially on the backhand; let it drop into the back corner, and it

could be fatal in winter. Watch Jonah Barrington for the best examples of the lob serve.

The lob serve requires three essential elements: height, width and no pace on the ball, so that it dies if allowed to drop in the back corner. To achieve height, strike the ball with a very open racket face, stroking up through the ball and aiming to hit the front wall a foot below the out-of-court line. To attain width angle the ball across court into the side wall, aiming just left of centre from the right box, and two thirds across from the left box, on the front wall. This brings the ball to strike the side wall just behind the service box and just below the out-of-court line, and makes it very difficult to deal with. Where pace is concerned, remember that if it is struck too hard, the ball rebounds off the back wall before bouncing, making it just as easy to deal with as in a short-length serve. Striking the serve with a very open face and hitting underneath the ball will help to float it up into the glare of the lights, making it twice as difficult to return, especially high on the backhand.

The lob serve is an often neglected shot at all levels of squash – work on it, perfect it and reap the reward.

Driven serve
The driven serve again aims to strike the side wall, though not as high as the lob serve, but its purpose is still to embarrass the 'hand-out' who is trying to return the ball safely. This serve is very often struck with cut or slice on the ball, which helps it to die once it bounces in the back corner. The driven serve is struck at about half to three-quarter pace, trying to cut the strings of the racket across the ball, and the target area is three quarters of the way up the front wall.

Hard-hit serve
Another service variation is the hard-hit serve, aimed, ideally, to strike the side-wall nick (the join between the floor and the side wall) just behind the back of the service box, or at least low on the side wall. This serve is struck with a flat racket face, to hit the front wall just above the cut line, giving 'hand-out' a low ball with pace on it to volley – a very difficult shot.

Corkscrew serve
Used sparingly, the corkscrew serve can be very effective as an element of surprise. Usually employed from the left-hand service box by right-handed players, it involves striking the ball so that it hits the front wall high up in the left-hand corner. The ball then hits the left-hand side wall and screws back across the court, ideally to strike the opposite side wall behind the back of the service box. If the ball is not volleyed by the receiver, it will bounce and run

along the back wall. Remember that with this, as with all serves, the ball must strike the front wall first. Any ball striking the side wall first will screw back in front of the short line and is a double fault.

Develop two serves to be your basics, such as the lob or semi-lob and the driven serve, then use the other variations sparingly, to catch your opponent by surprise. In this way, your serving will begin to become more consistent and also have a sting in the tail in the form of the variations.

Variations are useful to catch your opponent by surprise: try serving down the middle of the court, at his body, or a backhand serve. All these are designed to force a weak reply out of your opponent, making the game much easier for you to win.

Once you have served, don't stand admiring your effort but move quickly across to just behind the 'T', racket up, watching the ball and your opponent's racket, so you are ready to move to play the next shot. Your position in the service box, described earlier, will help your movement across to the 'T', so ensuring you are correctly placed and watching before your opponent strikes the return.

What happens on the rare occasions you have to return service? Remember that your opponent may have read this book as well!

The return of service is the key shot when 'hand-out' to gaining control of the rally. Its aim is to take your opponent away from the centre of the court, so that you can take up that position, snatching the initiative from the server. To achieve this, the ball should be hit to one of the four corners of the court, making your opponent travel away from the 'T' to return the ball.

For return of service, position yourself just behind the back corner of the service box, racket up, watching the server carefully. It is vital to watch the ball right from the moment of impact with the racket, to minimize the server's advantage. Adopt a slightly open-chested stance, so that it it easier for you to take the ball either on the forehand or backhand. With this position, it is far harder for 'hand-in' to catch you out with the serve down the middle of the court, or the serve at your body. However, do remember to be ready to move your feet – don't be caught 'flat-footed', expecting the serve to arrive on to your racket.

The safest return is to a length to the back of the court. This shot has the advantage not only of taking your opponent from the 'T', but also of putting him in a back corner with you in front in command. When you hit the ball straight to a length, there is less

Return of service

The ideal position to return service: racket up, open stance, ready to react to any service, standing just behind the back of the service box.

risk of it being cut off than with the cross-court return. The effectiveness of both shots depends on good width: it is no good pulling the shot away from the wall, giving your opponent an opportunity to intercept on the volley. With the length returns, straight or cross-court, a good-quality shot with width is the safest.

If your opponent out-thinks you, so that you are forced to let the ball drop into the back corner and you cannot straighten it, use the boast. This shot also takes your opponent away from the 'T', but unfortunately puts him in the front of the court in the 'driving seat' and in position to attack. When this happens, make life as difficult as possible for your opponent by using the defensive two-wall boast (see page 26). The moral is: only boast when *you* want to, not when your opponent forces you to.

Squash is like a chess game, in which each player tries to out-think the other, and nowhere is this more so than during the serve and return of service. 'Hand-in' is trying to force his opponent on to the defensive, to make him dig the ball out of the back corners – very difficult on a cold winter's night. It is a satisfying feeling to ace an opponent on service and very demoralizing for the receiver. 'Hand-out', meanwhile, is trying to take the initiative away from his opponent, by hitting the ball deep into the back corners. If you are receiving, try at all times to take the ball on the volley: step forwards to hit it early, rather than backwards, letting it drop.

If your opponent is causing you problems with his serve, do something positive about it, such as changing your position to return service – perhaps taking a step forward. Quite often this unsettles the server, who has got into a rhythm. What has been a near-perfect lob serve suddenly clips the line instead of striking the side wall just below it. The hard serve is a comfortable height to volley and the

Forehand Volley *Punch through the ball, striking it with an open racket opposite the leading shoulder.*

driven serve is now not close to the side wall, causing few problems for the attacking volleyer. Watch out for the crafty server who doesn't panic and hits the ball straight down the middle or at your body. Above all, be positive: go forward and don't retreat to return the ball.

Volley

The key to success in squash is the volley – taking the ball early, speeding up the game, applying pressure, making life particularly uncomfortable for your opponent. The basic volley, like the drive, is the length shot, keeping your opponent buried deep in the back of the court. Having forced him deep with good-quality length drives, quickly move in to take the ball on the volley, maintaining your dominance. The volley action is a much shorter swing than the drive, a punching action. There is no time to take a full swing at the ball – by the time you swing the racket through, the ball has gone past.

Forehand volley

From the ready position on the 'T', with the racket up, step across with the left foot, as for a drive. Ideally, the racket head should travel between the two o'clock and ten o'clock positions on an imaginary clock face, with a punched action. Strike the ball level with the leading shoulder, your racket face slightly open, your wrist firm and racket head up, and then follow through in the direction you want the ball to go.

Many times in a match it is not always possible to step across with the left foot. When volleying off the wrong foot, make sure that you turn your shoulders, so that they are parallel to the side wall: avoid playing the shot open-chested, as inevitably you drag

the ball away from the side wall and back towards you. When practising the volley, make sure that you learn to play the shot off either foot.

Backhand volley As with the forehand volley, from the ready position on the 'T' step across, this time with the right foot, as for a backhand drive. The swing is shorter, with the racket moving from ten o'clock to two o'clock on an imaginary clock face. Hit the ball slightly further forward than the leading shoulder, with a slightly open racket face, a firm wrist, and your racket head up and following through in the direction you want the ball to go. Use the other arm, uncrossing the arms as you strike the ball, to help control and power.

For the cross-court length volley, simply take the ball earlier, aiming to strike the opposite side wall around the back of the service box. The width of this cross-court shot obviously depends on the position of your opponent, so adjust your target area on the side wall accordingly.

Width is important for the volley if the advantage of taking the ball early is not to be lost. Ideally, the ball should travel on a downward trajectory from the front wall, putting even more pressure on your opponent as it gives him less time to recover to play an effective reply. The pushed volley, by having taken the ball early, does apply pressure; however, a volley with pace, width and length will bring greater dividends, making your opponent work harder. The key is length – taking the ball right to the back of the court, but not bouncing it a long way off the back wall. Watch Jahangir Khan, the arch exponent of this shot, who drives his opponent back with fierce volleys, eventually setting himself up for the kill.

The secret of good volleying is to keep the wrist firm and racket

Backhand Volley *As in the forehand use a punch-like action, firm wrist and open racket face.*

head up. If the wrist is floppy, the control of the racket head and therefore of the ball is affected, so producing a poor shot which lacks accuracy. If the ball is low, bend your knees to get down to it rather than dropping the racket head as this only results in loss of accuracy in the shot.

For forehand high volleys, use an overarm throwing action, still aiming to take the ball level with the leading shoulder. On the follow-through it is important not to let the wrist come over as this results in loss of length or even putting the ball into the tin if the wrist snaps over on impact. To ensure length on this shot, aim to strike the front wall high up.

When attempting a high backhand volley, hit through the ball, ensuring that the racket face continues in the direction you want the ball to go. Again, don't let the wrist snap over, otherwise loss of length and accuracy will result or even worse – the ball will go into the tin. As for the forehand, aim high up on the front wall to gain length.

As with the drives, transfer the body weight into the shot, whether the ball is played off the correct or the wrong foot. This helps to give the shot more bite and infinitely more control than if it is played leaning away from the ball. Be positive in the rallies: look for the ball to volley, hunt it in the air – don't just volley the ball that comes to you.

Angles

Boast

This shot is played either defensively from the back of the corner, when the ball cannot be straightened, or from the short-line back as an attacking shot to move your opponent to the front of the court.

Forehand Boast *The swing for the boast is as for the drive. Note the body position in relation to the ball. Strike the ball with an open racket face, aiming it into the side wall in the direction of the opposite front corner of an imaginary court next door.*

Only use the boast defensively as a last resort, because the shot can set your opponent up in the front of the court, giving him the whole court into which to play the ball. You must try to avoid allowing him to achieve this position as it gives him an opportunity to apply pressure. By forcing you to boast, through his good length and width, your opponent may find a weakness in your defences.

If there is no alternative other than to boast to return the ball, remember always to make your opponent play another shot. Don't hand the rally to him by hitting the tin and thereby lose the chance of setting him up. To avoid giving him the opportunity of an easy kill, use the two-wall boast. This shot hits the side wall nearest you, the front wall, then bounces in the opposite front corner, taking the ball in towards the side wall, making it very difficult to attack because of its proximity to the side wall.

The three-wall boast can be very effective if it either goes into

the nick in the opposite corner or hits the side wall low to the floor. However, it can, if not accurate, provide an opponent with an easy ball in the middle of the court to attack. The boast aiming to kill the ball is not a percentage shot: it carries an element of risk, like any other kill shot. Geoff Hunt occasionally used the three–wall boast to great effect, but by and large he used the two–wall shot to move his opponent up to the front of the court.

The swing for the boast is like that of the basic drive, with the exception of the body position in relation to the ball. From the basic drive position do a quarter turn, so that you are facing the back corner. The deeper the ball, the further you need to stay away from the side wall, giving yourself room to swing your racket. When playing a boast out of the back corner, don't plant your correct foot into the corner as this greatly restricts your swing, but go in first with the wrong foot and let the other foot catch up to form a solid

Backhand Boast *The same body position is required for the backhand corner, providing a solid base from which to play the shot. Remember to lift the ball up into the side wall, aiming to strike the wall above the height of an imaginary tin.*

base. Imagine there is a corridor around the court, about the width of the service box; don't get yourself completely in this corridor because it does not give you enough room to swing the racket.

As in the drive, the ball is struck with an open racket face up into the side wall opposite the leading foot. Aim to strike the ball so that, if it could travel through the side wall, it would end up in the opposite front corner of an imaginary court next door. It is useful to be able to picture the shot in your mind to help yourself achieve the correct angle.

Generally, whatever the height the ball is hit into the side wall is the height at which it strikes the front wall. (I say 'generally' because this is not true in all cases, but more about that later.) You should therefore imagine a tin running along the side wall and hit the ball into the wall above the height of the tin. Remember to bend your knees and back if the ball bounces low, and transfer your weight into the shot. If you fall away from the shot as you hit it – usually a result of getting too close to it – you lose control and the ball will strike the front wall too high.

There is no need to hit the ball at a hundred miles an hour to get it up: a half- or three-quarter-paced shot will suffice. The important thing to remember is to make sure you get the ball up. If the shot does not reach the front wall, you are striking the ball too late, having let it go past you, and the remedy is to take it earlier in relation to your body. On the other hand, if the ball is screwing back into the centre of the court, having hit the side wall too near the front wall, take the ball later. In both cases, picture in your mind striking the ball so that it would travel to the opposite front corner of a court next door.

Having played the boast shot, remember to recover from it – don't just stand at the back of the court, hoping your opponent will hit the ball back to you, but move up to just behind the 'T', so that you are in position to cover your opponent's next shot. The tighter your shot to the opposite front corner, drawing your opponent the maximum distance from the 'T', the more restricted he will be in his choice of shot. So, having been forced to boast by your opponent's good length and width, you have made the best of an awkward situation which could embarrass the incoming striker, forcing him to play a dying ball close to the side wall.

Practise your boast and turn what is a defensive shot into an attacking one. There is nothing more demoralizing than, having forced a defensive return from your opponent, finding yourself under pressure from the reply.

Let us now assume that you are in control of the rally and want to use the boast as an attacking shot, to move your opponent to the front of the court. (Remember that this is not a good idea at the start of a match when your opponent is fresh, as he will be able to reach the ball easily and attack it, putting you under pressure.) The boast as an attacking shot can be very effective in making your opponent run. It can be played from the short line, when in front of your opponent, or from the back of the court. Remember to use the boast from behind your opponent sparingly, as he is in front of you, on the 'T', ready to pounce.

As an attacking shot, the boast can be played either with or without pace. The soft floated boast is very effective, as the ball tends to die much more quickly than the incoming striker expects. The Egyptian Ahmed Safwat is an acknowledged master of this slow-paced boast. The shot does need to be lifted more into the side wall, otherwise it will hit the tin. Use a slightly more open racket face to help take the pace off the ball and apply cut to the shot. By the time the ball has hit the front wall, it should be dropping, so forcing the incoming striker to lift it in order to make a safe return. A hard-hit boast needs to be more accurate because, if over-hit, it tends to bounce up more, giving an opponent an easier ball to return. Both the hard and soft attacking boast are most effective when they strike two walls, forcing your opponent to play a ball right out of a front corner.

Remember that, when you have sent your opponent to the front of the court, move up ready to cut off any shot he hits to the back. In this way you can keep him on the move and maintain pressure. Use the attacking boast with discretion, the more so the higher the level of squash you play, as your opponent will tend to read the shot far more easily and be there waiting for the ball: the tables will be turned, with *you* under pressure, struggling to stay in the rally.

Volley boast

The boast shot can also be played on the volley, usually from the short line off a ball between knee and shoulder height. The aim of the shot is the same as that of any attacking shot, but with the added advantage of taking the ball early on the volley. It is best played when your opponent is behind you, when he is slow to move up from the back of the court, expecting a length volley. It is played like a volley, with a punching action and a slightly open racket face. Turn the shoulder towards the side wall, as the ball is struck slightly later than in the straight volley; and make sure your weight is transferred into the shot, otherwise control and accuracy are lost. It is vital only to play this as a variation when you are balanced –

don't use the shot when you are over-reaching and cannot recover from it quickly.

Other variations of the boast are the skid boast and the back-wall boast.

Skid boast The skid boast is a shot used to send the ball into the opposite back corner, via the side wall nearest you. As you are aiming to strike the ball into the side wall, your opponent naturally thinks the ball is going to the front of the court, but instead he finds it soaring over his head to the back. The shot is played by aiming to hit the ball higher up into the side wall and nearer the front wall. A more open racket face and uplift on the follow-through are required to achieve height to the shot. The ideal skid boast hits the opposite wall behind the back of the service box and then travels into the back corner. It can be an effective shot if used sparingly and when one is balanced, but is definitely not the shot to play when under pressure, hoping for a lucky winner by catching your opponent out.

Back-wall boast The back-wall boast is very useful, as a last resort, to return your opponent's good-length-and-width shot. If you are unable to straighten or boast your opponent's shot, use the back-wall boast. As its name suggests this shot uses the back wall to return the ball to the front wall and is an effective way of ensuring that your opponent has to play another shot. Facing the back wall, simply play a lob on to the back wall with a very open racket face, so floating the ball up over your head and on to the front wall. The diagonally played shot is more effective, as it gives you more time to recover and also takes the ball into a front corner. A ball dropping with very little pace on to the front wall, just over the tin and near the side wall, is difficult to deal with. Your opponent may well be tempted to try for an outright winner, as psychologically he feels he ought to be able to finish the rally off immediately, having forced you into a last-ditch reply. Very often he will make an error, giving you the chance to win the rally.

Make sure, having played the shot, that you move up the court to cover not only the drop, but also the straight and cross-court drives. An effective way of dealing with the back-wall boast is to delay your shot as long as possible, then simply hit either a straight or cross-court length shot which, if hit with good width, catches many an opponent out. If you can take the ball early on the volley, try the drop volley which doesn't give your opponent as much time to recover from the back of the court.

The back-wall boast should really be employed only as a last-resort: don't get into the habit of using it at the expense of trying to straighten or boast the ball. Hiddy Jahan uses the shot a great deal, quite often playing it from just behind the short line when caught out by cross-court drives, hitting it hard on to the back wall. However, it is not a good habit to get into, unless you are a world-class player!

The boast at the front of the court is called the 'angle' or 'trickle' boast. This shot is played as an alternative to the straight drop shot and, as with the drop, it is played with an open racket face. Strike the ball late, making it hit the side wall nearest you first, then the front wall. Play the shot softly, so that the ball does not rebound too far out into the middle of the court. The shot can also be hit hard off a ball bouncing above the height of the tin, the aim being to take it into the opposite front corner. Both shots can be used as alternatives to the straight drop, but try not to use them too often or your opponent may start to read them early. If this happens, he will be on to the ball, hitting it away to the back of the court and leaving you stranded, still trying to recover to the 'T'. Used sparingly, they can be effective as a variation, catching your opponent flat-footed.

The angle

The reverse angle is a variation on the basic side-wall shot and its aim is to hit the ball on to the side wall farthest away from you. The ball then travels across the front wall to strike the wall in the opposite front corner.

Reverse angle

Play the shot when balanced, having worked your opponent out of position off a loose ball and ending up in the middle of the court with him trapped behind you on the opposite side from that on which the ball eventually ends up. Because the shot is being played across your body, take the ball earlier as you would for a cross-court drive, aiming your feet and shoulders in the direction in which you want the ball to go. Ideally this shot should come back across the court to hit the side wall nick in the front corner. A variation used by some, notably Jamie Hickox the young Surrey player, is to play the shot from behind your opponent, off a loose length drive, aiming to deceive him. This type of reverse angle tends to be played so that the ball strikes the side wall and then the front wall, dying towards the centre of the court rather than played to end up in the front corner.

Again, be careful not to over-use this shot. Employed sparingly, it can be a very deceptive weapon, but if your opponent grows to expect it, it can set him up for the kill, especially if hit too high over the tin. It is a risky shot, especially when played from in front of your opponent, as the ball comes back to your side of the court, so be sure to clear it well to avoid giving a 'stroke' away.

Lob The lob is a most under-used shot at all levels of squash, players preferring the hard-hit low cross-court shot to extricate themselves from trouble. Basically, the lob is used as a defensive shot, giving you time to recover to the centre of the court when under pressure. It can also be used very effectively as an attacking weapon against an opponent who likes a fast pace on the ball to hit. If you were lucky enough to watch the artful Pakistani Gogi Alauddin, the master exponent of the lob, in his heyday, you would have seen him floating the ball around the court and frustrating his opponents into making errors. Jonah Barrington still uses the lob to great effect under pressure, flicking the ball up over his opponent into the back of the court.

The lob can either be played straight or cross-court, both shots requiring two elements: height and width.

Straight lob The straight lob is very similar in its execution to the drive. However, the ball is struck slightly further forward, with a very open racket face off a good wide base, having taken a long last stride, reaching for the ball. With the follow-through, bring the racket head up more than on the drive: this, combined with the very open racket face, gives height to the shot. Aim high up on the front wall. Stay down with the shot, otherwise the ball is pushed over the side-wall out-of-court line. There is less margin for error with the straight shot: it should be glued to the side wall and high enough

so that it cannot be reached by an eager volleyer. The ball should drop deep in the back corner, making it very difficult to return with anything other than a defensive reply.

The cross-court lob, as with the straight shot, requires both height and width. The ball should hit the front wall high up in the middle, aiming to strike the side wall just below the out-of-court line and behind the back of the service box, bouncing in the back corner and forcing a defensive reply from your opponent. It is vital that this shot has width as well as height, so that it cannot be cut off.

To achieve the width, the ball is played earlier than in the straight shot. With a very open racket face, reach for it with a long last stride and use more uplift on the follow-through than for the drive. As with the straight lob, stay down: don't come up too early with the follow-through, or the ball may go out over the side-wall out-of-court line.

A good lob should be floated high and wide, away from any eager opponent looking to cut the ball off on the volley. Try to take as much pace off the ball as possible by using a very open racket face, lifting the ball up rather than hitting it.

Remember: when under pressure at the front of the court, use the lob to give yourself time to recover to the 'T' and, at the same time, turn the tables on your opponent by putting him on the defensive in a back corner.

The lob can be used equally effectively from the back of the court. Avoid simply trying to hit your way out when in trouble behind your opponent. This often leads to more problems, as a short-length reply gives an eager opponent a chance to attack still

Cross-court lob

Forehand Cross-Court Lob
Take the ball earlier than for the straight drive to achieve width. Strike the ball with a very open racket face to give height to the shot.

Backhand Cross–Court Lob As with the forehand shot, note the long last stride where the player is reaching for the ball, the low body position, and the uplift on the follow–through to help give height to the shot.

further, sending the ball short. If the shot is hit cross–court, very often poor width gives your opponent an opportunity to cut the ball off short in the opposite front corner.

Instead of trying to hit harder and lower to remove the presssure on you, use height on the front wall to pass your opponent. Like the lob from the front of the court, this shot needs both height and width to float the ball either straight or cross–court over your opponent's head. To help ensure that your shot is not cut out on the volley, picture target areas on the front wall. These will assist you in stroking the ball with sufficient height and width to elude an eager volleyer on the 'T'. Imagine a newspaper hanging from the out–of–court line on the front wall, right up against the side wall for the straight shot, or in the middle of the front wall for the cross–court shot: these are the targets at which you should aim; and the better you are, the smaller the target areas can be.

Remember: if you are under pressure, use the full height and width of the court to turn defence into attack. Learn to use the lob intelligently to frustrate your opponent.

Drop There are two reasons for playing the drop shot: to try to win the rally outright and to make your opponent run to the front of the court. When should you play this shot? Basically, look for the weak reply that bounces in front of the short line with your opponent deep in the court, out of position. By attacking with good-quality length and width, set up opportunities to use the drop to win the rally. It is not a shot to play when under pressure and off balance, but when you are in control of the rally, having worked your opponent out of position.

The swing for the drop is similar to the basic swing for the forehand and backhand drives. Prepare early for the shot, making it look as though you are going to play a drive and keeping your opponent guessing. The footwork is the same: lead with the left foot for the forehand and with the right foot for the backhand. It is important for the shot on both sides of the court to step across to play the drop, so turning the shoulders. This helps you to guide the ball towards the front corner of the court. If you step towards the front wall, you have to push the shot towards the corner, which often causes loss of accuracy or even a miss-hit, with the ball going down.

Straight drop

From the preparation position, the difference between the drop and the drive is that the racket head slows down rather than speeds up through the hitting area. The drop at the front of the court should be played with a very open racket face, slowing the racket head down through the impact area, to develop a soft touch to the shot. Strike the ball at the top of its bounce with a touch of cut, which is given by the very open racket face cutting the strings across the back of the ball.

Aim the drop shot to hit the front wall an inch or two above the tin, angling the ball in so that it hits the side-wall nick, or at least low on the side wall, before bouncing. It is important that the ball does strike two walls before it bounces. As the ball is struck softly to begin with, the impact on two walls before bouncing takes more pace off it so it will not bounce very much at all. This makes it difficult for your opponent to do anything but lift the ball, giving you a chance to volley it, keeping the pressure on him.

On the drop shot, remember to follow through, though not as much as with the drive. This is important; otherwise you will poke at the ball with disastrous results – either failing to reach the front

Forehand Drop *The swing for the drop is similar to that for the drive. Note the very open racket face on impact and the shorter follow-through.*

wall or striking it far too high, giving your opponent an easy opportunity to play the ball to the back of the court for a winner, with you out of position.

As the drop is a delicate shot, not leaving much margin for error, it is most important to have a good balanced base, keeping the head and shoulders still throughout, to minimize the chance of error. Having worked for the opening to play the drop, don't waste it: take care over the shot and don't 'run away' from it, but finish it off before recovering to the 'T'.

When moving back to the 'T', having played a drop from the front of the court, don't back straight to the 'T' on a diagonal. This will almost certainly obstruct your opponent, blocking his way to the ball. Remember that it is up to you to allow an unobstructed path to the ball and not up to your opponent to go round you. The correct movement pattern is to push off back towards the opposite

side wall, then back to the 'T' in an 'L'-shaped movement. (See the section on court movement on page 51.)

The drop at the front of the court requires a great deal of practice to acquire the soft touch which makes it effective. If playing the shot when going for an outright winner, your target area on the front wall is lower, but still allow yourself some margin for error. When playing the drop to move your opponent forward, you can afford to aim higher on the front wall. Remember that, when using this shot, it is only going to be as good as the quality of your length. The deeper you bury your opponent in the back of the court, the more time you are going to have to play the shot because there is more court between the ball and your opponent. This means that the shot does not have to be so tight to the tin, and with less pressure on the striker, there is less chance of an error. One of the important elements of a good drop is that it doesn't rebound too far

Backhand Drop *As with the forehand drop, note the balanced position and how the head and shoulders are kept still throughout the shot. Note the preparation: if you have time this helps deception.*

Forehand Cross-Court Drop
This shot is played like the straight drop, except that the ball is taken earlier as in all cross-court shots.

from the front wall. Practise with a target on the floor and aim to hit it or bounce the ball in front of it.

Frequently, with the drop at the front, there isn't time to prepare as for a drive, the shot being played at full stretch. Keep the racket face open, getting underneath the ball with a firm wrist. This is often a shot played as a counter-drop as your opponent recovers to the 'T', so catching him out. Even though at full stretch, remember to be balanced and still, and don't present your opponent with the rally by hitting the tin.

Cross-court drop

The cross-court drop shot can be an effective variation to the straight drop, or it can be disastrous, offering an eager opponent an easy opportunity to win the rally. The shot should be played to hit the side-wall nick on the opposite side of the court, or at least strike the side wall low down before it bounces. Any shot that doesn't get

the required width is a sitting target to be put away for a winner.

As in the straight drop, use a very open racket face to apply cut, slowing the racket head down through the impact area and with a shorter follow-through than for the drive. Impact for the cross-court shot is earlier than for the straight shot. Make sure that you take the ball out in front of your body, floating it across the front wall and aiming to hit an imaginary racket head a racket's length from the side wall. The exact target area on the front wall depends on where you are playing the shot: experiment during practice so that you learn to picture in your mind where to aim.

As with all shots, it is vital to get down to the ball, bending the knees and the back. Don't play the shot upright like a statue, just dropping the racket head, as this only leads to poor shot production and a bad end result. A balanced striking position is important, keeping head and shoulders still: any over-rotation of the upper

Backhand Cross-Court Drop
Remember to play the shot with a very open racket face. Note the similarity to the backhand straight drop.

body affects the shot.

The straight and cross-court shots described so far should be played with the objective of achieving a soft touch on the drop. This is the shot to use when in the front third of the court, carefully guiding the ball into the front corners and aiming for the side-wall nick. The nearer the ball bounces to the front wall, the further your opponent is going to have to run to pick up the shot.

It is vital to be positive. Play a shot with a shorter follow-through – don't be tentative, as this is when errors can creep in and you lose confidence in the drop. If your opponent is reaching your drops easily, perhaps you are not driving him deep enough before playing them or you are using them too early in the match when he is fresh.

The drop can also be played from any length in the court, but remember that it is not a shot to use when off balance and under pressure. Wait until you are in control of the rally and have eliminated risks. The further back from the front wall the shot is played, the greater the possibility of an error.

There are many variations on the straight and cross-court drop played at the front of the court, and these are considered below.

Variations to the drop

The further from the front wall the drop is played, the more cut needed to control the shot. The cut on the drop has two effects. First, the ball does not travel so slowly to the front wall. With the floated drop, played from deeper in the court, the ball is in the air longer, giving your opponent more time to reach it. Second, the cut drop tends to die quicker, because the cut has the effect of making the ball bounce lower.

Like the drop at the front of the court, the cut drop is best played when you are balanced and in control of the rally, not when you are under pressure and just hoping for a lucky winner. Take the ball at the top of its bounce – preferably a ball that has bounced above the height of the tin, though it is possible to impart cut to a low-bouncing ball. Instead of hitting through it, as for the drive, bring the open racket face down the back of the ball, then continue forwards. This has the effect of imparting cut to the ball so that, after bouncing, it does not sit up but stays down. This is why the Pakistanis, in particular Qamar Zaman, have been so effective: even their length drives don't tend to rebound so far off the back wall as a result of this stroking action.

This drop is often played very effectively from half- or three-quarter court off poor length drives. The footwork and other aspects of the drop are nearly the same as in the drive. As the shot is often played off a ball that bounces above the tin, a more upright body position is required (remember to bend if playing the shot off a low-bouncing ball), though still transfer your weight into the shot with your head still, and don't pull away from the ball. By cutting down the back of the ball, you can aim to hit it on a downward trajectory without closing the racket face, so minimizing the chances of error.

Aim to strike the front wall two or three inches above the tin to give yourself some margin for error. You can afford to aim higher, as the ball tends to die quicker. The further from the side wall you play this shot, the wider the angle you have, so you can aim for the side-wall nick. Even should you miss the side wall, if the ball is kept tight to the wall, bouncing low, it is a very difficult shot to attack and can be useful against a hard-hitting player.

Forehand Drop using cut *The important point to note with this shot is to cut the strings down the back of the ball.*

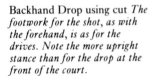

Backhand Drop using cut *The footwork for the shot, as with the forehand, is as for the drives. Note the more upright stance than for the drop at the front of the court.*

The cut drop can be played off low ground strokes by bending the knees to get down to the ball. Jahangir Khan is a good model to follow here. At impact, his wrist is still cocked, keeping the racket head up and maintaining good racket-head control. In this way, he is able to attack his opponent's poor length shots with the heavily cut drop. The secret is to be confident and strike through the ball, letting the racket strings work for you.

This shot can be played very effectively off over-hit length shots. Choose the ball carefully, however: don't try to play the shot off a tight ball close to the side wall as this is asking for trouble. The shot is often effective against an opponent who tends to hang back, not moving up to the 'T' after hitting a length shot. Obviously, it is also another means of moving your opponent forward and, by cutting the ball, you can make it die quicker, forcing a defensive reply from your opponent.

The shot is played to strike the front wall, then the side-wall nick, or at least kept tight to the side wall, restricting the choice of return. Again, use the racket strings to impart cut by drawing the racket head underneath the ball through the impact area. If played with the same preparation as for the drive, it is a difficult shot to spot.

The drop shot, using cut, can be played either straight or cross-court, but the important point to remember is that you must be in a balanced position when attempting to play it, even though there is less chance of error than with the floated shot because the cut drop is played with a very open racket face. If attempting a cross-court shot, take the ball earlier.

The Pakistanis use a variation of this cut drop at the front of court, off loose boast shots, to great effect. The shot involves moving

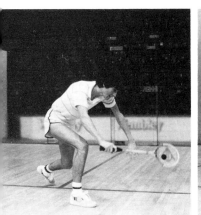

on to the ball quickly, playing it as your opponent is still recovering from the back of the court. Instead of playing the soft pushed drop, they cut the ball wide back across court, aiming for the side wall just in front of the short line on the second bounce. By cutting the ball, you will tend to keep it down, forcing your opponent to twist and turn while trying to recover it as it dies tight to the side wall. The shot does not have to be hit hard, but you should concentrate on taking it early and cutting it wide across the court.

Jahangir Khan cuts the ball wide across his opponent's body to great effect from half- and three-quarter court, making his opponent twist and turn wickedly. In the final of the 1983 ICI Perspex World Masters at Warrington, against Qamar Zaman, in one rally – off balls bouncing in the service box – he cut the ball wide across Zaman's body, aiming second bounce for the opposite side wall at the back of the service box. This was an extremely difficult shot to retrieve, as the ball didn't bounce, forcing Zaman to lift it. He was not able to hit a good length, giving Jahangir another opportunity to cut the ball back across court, first to forehand, then to backhand. Zaman was forced to twist, turn and bend low to retrieve the ball, first one way and then the other, which sapped the strength from his legs.

The same effect can also be achieved by taking early an opponent's attempted length drive from the front half of the court, cutting the ball across his body on the volley. Aim the shot wide on the second bounce for the opposite side wall, towards the back of the service box. Again, this forces your opponent to an awkward twisting and turning movement to recover your shot.

These are advanced ideas that need much practice to perfect, either on your own or with a partner, so set the ball up and have a go. They are variations which should not be over-used, but should be played when the right opportunities arise while you are balanced and in command of the rally. Once mastered, these shots can be extremely effective weapons in your armoury.

Drop volley This shot is very useful to cut off your opponent's drives or lobs, to move him to the front of the court, or played as a winner. The aim is to take the pace off the ball and drop it into one of the two front corners, either straight or cross-court. It is a shot not widely used at club level, most players preferring to volley hard and low.

Imagine a rally up and down the side wall, both players probing for an opening to attack. This kind of rally does not take very much out of either player, especially if neither is looking to volley the ball to apply pressure. One player tends to hang back, expecting the length drive, and this is the moment to move in, taking the ball early on the volley and playing the drop volley to make your opponent run the full length of the court to return it. This sometimes results in an outright winner, catching your opponent by surprise. If your opponent does reach the ball, he is forced to lift it with you behind him, ready to pounce, looking again to volley the ball deep and sending him off on another long run to the back of the court.

A variation which you can try occasionally is to play the ball short again, making your opponent move quickly forward, but only do this if you've sent him deep or otherwise he may be waiting for the short shot. So in the space of two or three shots, you have turned a gentle length rally into a mad scramble for survival by your opponent, making him work really hard to stay in it. A few more rallies like this and you will slowly draw the sting out of your

opponent: he will become impatient, trying to finish the rallies off quickly and making errors as fatigue takes over.

To play the drop volley, you should look for a loose width ball between knee and head height, or just above. If you have to over-reach to play the shot, you have chosen the wrong ball: the risk of error increases the more you have to reach for the ball because this lessens your control of the racket head. As when going for any shot, you must be balanced.

The preparation for the shot is the same as for the length volley. For the forehand, step across into the shot with the left foot; for the backhand, with the right foot. Play the ball for the straight shot in line with the leading shoulder on the forehand and just in front of it on the backhand. You are aiming to drop the ball two or three inches over the tin, close to the side wall. The further away from the side wall you are when playing the shot, the more you should try to angle the ball to hit the front wall, then the side wall. Ideally, as with the drop shot, you are aiming for the nick. The nearer to the side wall you are, the tighter you should keep your shot to the wall, making it very difficult for your opponent to do anything other than put the ball back into play.

As in the drop shot, slow the racket face down through the impact area. Combine this with playing the shot, using a very open racket face and taking the pace off the ball. Be positive: don't just let the ball hit the strings but take the racket face to it. The effect of this is like the ground-stroke drop – just poking at the ball causes errors. It is a soft shot, requiring a great deal of racket-head control. Keep the wrist firm and the racket head up. A floppy wrist means loss of control, very often sending the shot into the tin. Another very common fault with the drop volley is looking where the shot is

Forehand Drop Volley *Use a very open racket with the cutting action. Keep the wrist firm to aid racket-head control.*

Backhand Drop Volley *Be positive when playing the drop volley. Maintain a balanced position and keep the head still. Note the footwork, as for the backhand volley.*

going as you strike the ball: keep your head still and your eye on the ball to minimize the chances of error.

Earlier the technique of cutting the ball to help make it die was discussed. With the drop volley, use the same method. Watch Jonah Barrington or Jahangir Khan in action and listen to the noise of the strings cutting across the back of the ball. Off a ball at waist height or above, the path of the racket face should be down on an imaginary clock face from about two o'clock to eight for the forehand and ten o'clock to four for the backhand, cutting down the back of the ball. For any ball lower than waist height, the cutting action need not be so pronounced as the very open racket face helps to impart some cut. This shot does have a follow-through, like the drop.

Remember: be positive. Picture your target area on the front wall,

imagine a racket head in the front corners and aim for it. Above all, be balanced when going for the shot. If the ball is below waist height, bend the knees to play the shot: don't just drop the racket head because you lose control this way and increase the likelihood of making an error.

This shot can also be played cross-court as a variation when you have worked your opponent out of position. Imagine a racket lying along the top of the tin with the handle in the corner; your target area is again the racket head. The aim of the cross-court shot is to hit front wall in the opposite corner and then the side-wall nick, or at least a point low down on the side wall. Remember that if the ball hits two walls, each takes more pace off the ball so that it dies quicker and any reply has to be lifted.

Forehand Cross-Court Volley
Like the straight drop volley, except take the ball earlier.

Backhand Cross-Court Volley
In all other respects the cross-court drop volley is as for the straight drop volley, except the ball is taken earlier. If the cross volley is to be hit hard, the shot is the same, except that the racket head travels faster through the impact area.

The shot, like any other cross-court shot, is played earlier and further in front than for the straight shot. Play it with slice, keeping the racket face open, the wrist firm, and the racket head up for good control. Just as with the straight drop volley, use a cutting action, bringing the racket down and also across the flight path of the ball.

Go on to court, experiment with the straight and cross-court drop volleys, but more about practising later.

Kill This is a spectacular, exciting shot which sets packed galleries gasping. A kill is a high-risk shot in which there is very little room for error. It requires much practice before it can be played with confidence in a match.

The object of a kill is to hit the ball hard, aiming into the side wall nick at the front of the court. There are two types of kill: ground strokes, i.e. hit after the bounce; or volleys taken early. Both sorts can be hit either straight or cross-court off loose returns from your opponent from around the short line, when you have worked him out of position. Play kills off balls away from the side wall on the straight shots so that you have an angle, enabling you to aim into the nick. When you are going for the cross-court shot, the nearer the ball to side wall when attempting the kill, the greater the chance of your making an error.

Ground-stroke kill This shot is played very similarly to the normal forehand and backhand drive. Look for a loose ball in the front half of the court, away

from the side wall, bouncing above the height of the tin. (This last point is important, because to kill the ball you need to hit down.) Don't make the mistake of playing a kill with a closed racket face, as this increases the risk of hitting the tin – music to the ears of your opponent. Use an open racket face and hit down the back of the ball, effectively heavily cutting the ball as a drop from half-court but aiming to hit it hard. Remember to turn a little more than for the drives for both the straight forehand and backhand kills, so that it is easier to aim the ball to strike the front wall, then into the side-wall nick about a yard from the front wall.

When playing the cross-court kill, take the ball earlier out in front of you as in the cross-court drive. Aim at the front wall, then into the side-wall nick, as for the straight shot. Again, look for a ball bouncing above tin height and hit down with an open racket face, which minimizes the chances of making an error.

The same straight and cross-court kills can be played on the volley. **Volley kill** Look for a loose ball around about shoulder height or just above, away from the side wall. Any ball for which you have to over-reach is not the one to choose for these shots. Usually the volley kills are played from around the short line or just behind: the deeper you are, the more likelihood there is of your making an error.

The straight volley kill is played like the drop volley, aiming to strike the ball into the side-wall nick so that it rolls along the floor. Use a throwing action with the racket head for the forehand, as if you were trying to throw the ball into the front corner of the court.

To get the feel of this, stand on the short line by the edge of the service box and actually throw the ball down into the front corner. Once you are accustomed to the action required, feed up an easy ball and throw the racket head through at the ball. Ensure that you adopt a side-on position, stepping across with your left foot. On the backhand, use an open racket face, keeping the wrist cocked, so the racket head stays up, striking down through the ball. Don't snap the wrist over; some shots may go up, but the majority will go into the tin. Adopt a sideways position, stepping across with the right foot into the shot.

On the cross-court volley kill, aim to take the ball earlier, striking it out in front of you. For the forehand cross-court volley kill, practise the throwing action technique without a racket first of all to help yourself gain an idea of where to aim the ball on to the front wall. The backhand action is as for the straight shot, but again taking the ball earlier. Try to avoid snapping the wrist over in an attempt to achieve more power: accuracy is far more important. The backhand straight and cross-court volley kills are two of the hardest shots to play in squash, so don't be down-hearted if you are unable to master them immediately.

Choosing the right ball off which to play kill shots is all-important, because there is a high risk element in going for them. Work for the opening to play the kill, then act positively. Wait until you are balanced, relax and stroke the racket head through the ball for the ground strokes, and throw it through for the volley kills. Above all, practise. This is the only way to be certain that when the opportunity comes for kill shots during a game, you will play them successfully.

Summary   In squash there is no such thing as one correct technique, but there are many variations. You have only to look at the world's top players to realize that. What is important is to have a sound basic technique that can withstand pressure in a match. This section on stroke production is intended to give you an insight into the basic and, in some cases, more advanced technique for hitting a squash ball.

Hiddy Jahan, the world-ranked English international, said in a recent squash programme on television that he believes it is important to learn a sound basic technique. As your game progresses, you can then adopt your own personal style. The important thing is to have a sound stroke technique that does not break down under pressure. The less complicated your basic swing, the less chance of this happening in match play.

Playing the game

2

All great squash players have one thing in common: they move well around court. They don't run, but appear to glide across the surface. This apparently effortless movement gives them time to play the ball, an ability all great sportsmen and sportswomen have, no matter what their sport. Jahangir Khan, the current world champion, is a good example.

Develop good movement around the court to help improve your own game. Mistakes are often made as a result of arriving too late and in the wrong position to play the ball. Poor movement restricts your choice of shots, the classic example being to run straight towards the ball in a front corner, so being able to hit only cross-court.

Consider first movement to and from the 'T' to the four corners of the court. Don't run diagonally into the corners as this only cramps you for room, restricting your shot selection. Next, to help yourself improve your movement, try taking a fresh look at the court. You know that the walls restrict your swing, especially if you get too near to them, so imagine a corridor, the width of the service box, all around the edge of the court. Regard this as no man's land and try to put only one foot in it, so keeping yourself further away from the ball.

The initial movement from the 'T' to the front corners of the court should be straight to the front wall, then step across towards the ball with either the left or right foot, depending on whether you are playing a forehand or a backhand shot. In other words it is an 'L'-shaped movement, helping you to arrive in the right position with the ball to the side of your body to strike it. The movement to the back of the court is along a similarly 'L'-shaped path which takes you down the middle of the court then across towards the ball.

A well-executed recovery from a corner to the 'T' is just as important: first, so that you don't impede your opponent; and second, so that you recover to the 'T' area balanced, with your racket up, watching before your opponent strikes the ball. The initial movement from a front corner is towards the opposite side wall, then back to the 'T', with your eye on the ball at all times.

Court movement

Court movement pattern showing the path to and from the 'T' area.

This movement pattern gives your opponent a clear pathway to the ball. From a back corner, first of all move towards the half-court line, then up to the 'T' area. From either a front or back corner the movement takes the form of a reverse 'L'-shape.

When moving to play the ball, employ this pattern of up then across for any ball in front of the short line, and back and across for any ball behind the short line. When playing a ball on or around the short line, simply step across and recover straight back to the 'T' area, assuming you don't hit the ball down the middle of the court, back to yourself.

Good movement around the court can be learnt in the same way as can the technique of hitting a squash ball. Start with the basics and gradually build up until you are working at speed. Initially quality of movement is far more important than speed; you will only accentuate bad habits if you attempt to get quicker too soon.

The best way of improving your movement is to do an exercise called 'ghosting', made famous by Jonah Barrington, which involves playing squash without the ball. Move to the corners of the court, play a shadow stroke, then recover to the 'T'. Two things are vital if this form of training is to have any value: first, move correctly to and from each corner, concentrating on good footwork; and second, play a correct stroke – don't just swing the racket as though you were swatting a fly. Recovery back to the 'T' is important: remember to watch the imaginary ball behind you. Don't just run through the 'T'; avoid running straight diagonals corner to corner, but always incorporate changes of direction in your ghosting.

By watching a game of squash, it is possible to plot where most of the shots are played from. Incorporate this information in your ghosting routine, bearing in mind the movement pattern to and from the ball described earlier. In the illustration ten areas on the court floor are numbered to represent the areas to which you can move, playing an imaginary shot at each. Vary the stroke played so at (1) and (2) it could be a drive, drop or lob; the same at (3) and (4); at (5) and (6) a drive, low or high volley; a drive, boast or volley at (7) and (8); and at (9) and (10) a drive or boast. The important point to bear in mind is to play a proper stroke – don't just waft your racket in the air.

Footwork is very important, so try to be balanced when playing a stroke at the ball and then push off to recover back to the 'T'. For positions (1) to (4), concentrate on correct footwork: left foot across for the forehand, right for the backhand. For positions (6) and (8) on the forehand side, most top players play the ball off what is technically called the 'wrong' foot. The reason for this is to make it easier and quicker to recover to the 'T'. Remember, though, to be balanced and turn the shoulders so that you are still and side-on when playing the ball. On the backhand side – numbers (5) and (7) – top players again step across with the wrong foot for speed.

Numbered stations for ghosting sessions to train good movement.

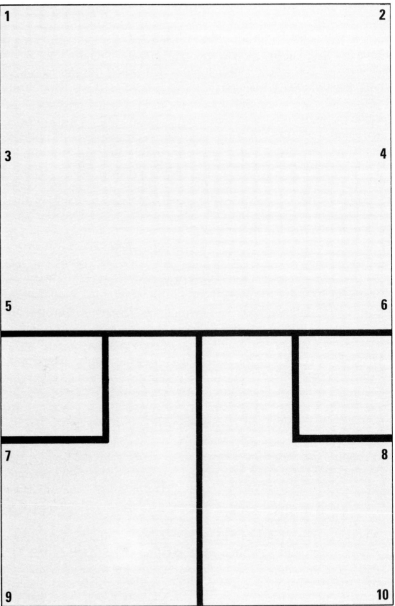

Initially for areas (9) and (10) reach in with the wrong foot first and let the other catch up to make a balanced position – this means the right foot on the forehand side and left foot on the backhand side of the court. You will thus have much more room to swing the racket at the ball, so enabling you to keep your options open to play straight, cross-court or boast. Stepping into the back corners with technically the 'correct' foot restricts your choice of shots.

Quality is very important when ghosting. Don't just dash around the court but start slowly to groove your movement, just as you would when learning to play a stroke. Gradually increase the pace at which you move, using the interval-training formula of equal work/rest periods (see page 100) and counting the number of repetitions you do in each work period. Ghosting can also be used for speed training, employing the explosive speed formula of ten seconds' work, fifty seconds' rest. It is a good idea to work in pairs with one player working while the other rests, calling out the numbers as the 'worker' recovers to the 'T'. It is helpful to place cards on the court floor, numbering the areas, especially to begin with.

Incorporate ghosting into your training programme and, over a period of weeks, if you have paid attention to detail when doing it, there should be a marked improvement in your movement around court. This should have two effects: first, you start returning balls more accurately and even retrieving shots you previously were unable to do; and second, because your movement is more economical, you waste less energy. The net result is a better performance in your match play. Squash players often spend a lot of time hitting

Jahangir Khan (Pakistan), the World No. 1, demonstrating a good balanced position to straighten the ball out of the back corner. Note the position of the feet, giving the player room to make an unrestricted shot. (Photograph: Stephen Line)

a ball, which is obviously very important, but, in doing so, they neglect their court movement training. Make ghosting part of your training programme and you'll be delighted with the improvement.

Deception   Deception is an important element in the game of squash. If you become totally predictable, then you are easier to beat. Some players are naturally deceptive: Hiddy Jahan, Qamar Zaman and Dean Williams spring to mind.

While it is good to use some deception in your game, don't become obsessed with it. Any deception is only as effective as the

Gamal Awad (Egypt) showing his brand of deception. (Photograph: Robin Eley Jones)

basic percentage shot from that position in the court. The more you play the basic shot, the more effective the deception is likely to be. Remember the key to any deception is time: you must arrive early enough to set yourself up, balanced, to create the opportunity to deceive.

Deception can be employed from anywhere in the court, but is probably most effective from the back of the service box forward. (Zaman, however, uses deception from anywhere in the court.)

In the front of the court, the key is to arrive early, so that you have the time to hold the shot. The longer you can hold your racket before hitting the ball, the longer the time your opponent has to think and commit himself as to where the ball is going. So arrive early, racket up; stop, then play the ball. Work with a partner, playing the drive boast routine, with the proviso that the person at the front can hit either straight or cross-court. See if you can send each other the wrong way when at the front of the court.

The second form of deception is to use your wrist. Hiddy Jahan is an expert at this. On the backhand, with apparently the same action, he can play the most delicate of drop volleys or volley hard and low to the back, simply by a flick of the wrist. He employs the same technique for the backhand drop or hard cross-court drive. You need a very strong, supple wrist to be able to emulate him.

Another variation of this is to take the ball very late, breaking the wrist at the last second to send the ball in the opposite direction. Your opponent should then be off chasing thin air.

The use of the wrist is a more difficult technique to employ for deception. You need to experiment during practice so that you become aware of what the racket head is doing and learn to break the wrist fractionally as late as possible.

Another legitimate form of deception is to mask the ball with your body, preventing your opponent from actually seeing you hit it. In that fraction of a second when your body is between him and the ball, he loses time to move to play his shot, enabling you to deceive him. Remember, though, when you have played the ball, to give your opponent a clear path to it – don't stand on the shot.

Deception is often very effective from half- to three-quarter court. Again, use the stop/hold technique with a high preparation or even a long racket swing from knee height, then play the ball. By doing this, you are trying to commit your opponent to go one way before you put the ball the other. Jahangir Khan has good deception on the forehand; at times you think that at best he can only hit straight from his position, but then he whips the ball, heavily cut cross-court, past a stranded opponent.

The ideal set-up for deception, holding the shot, demonstrated by Ross Norman (New Zealand). (Photograph: Stephen Line)

Opportunities for deception in squash are set up by a sound basic game, based on length and width. These two elements must be the basis on which to build deception into your game. There is nothing more satisfying than sending an opponent the wrong way.

Developing your game

Having worked hard at improving your stroke technique, how can you develop your game? It is not enough simply to look good on a squash court; you have to be able not only to apply pressure to your opponent, but to withstand it as well.

In squash, whatever your level, rallies are rarely won easily, unless playing against a much weaker opponent. You need to make your opponent work hard, keeping him running, moving him around the court, and in this way open up an opportunity to play a winner.

Squash has often been likened to chess. However, unlike chess, squash is both a mental and a physical game. A squash player who doesn't use his brain will win up to a certain level, but then struggle to make further progress.

The following sections look at the basic theory, the fundamental principles of the game.

What is meant by 'good length', a term often used in squash? A good length shot is one that takes your opponent away from the centre of the court, making him travel into one of the back corners to play his next shot, forcing him on the defensive and, if you are lucky, making him boast the ball. Learn to use length to your advantage whether playing a drive, volley or lob, to set up opportunities to play a winner.

Remember: it is no good just aimlessly hitting the ball as hard as possible to the back of the court as it will bounce a long way off the back wall, putting no pressure on your opponent. The length shot must bury him in the 'graveyard' – the back corners of the court – applying maximum pressure and forcing a weak reply from him. Attack and defend through keeping the ball deep and your opponent behind you. The use of the length shot is especially important early on in a match. Keep driving the ball deep to draw the strength out of your opponent, to soften him up physically as well as mentally. Imagine playing Barrington or Hunt in their heyday: their relentless length kept forcing their opponents back into the 'graveyard', which must have been very dispiriting.

When playing the ball to length, balanced and not under pressure, whether at the front or back of the court, try to impart pace to the shot. This has the effect of making your opponent move quickly, at or near-maximum pace, to return the ball. If this pressure can be kept up, it soon begins to wear down an opponent. Jahangir Khan, the world champion, is a very good exponent of the pressurized game, as are two former holders of the same title, Geoff Hunt and Jonah Barrington.

Length is the key to success in squash.

It is very important that, to complement good length, you keep the ball out of reach of your opponent. Don't let him cut your attempted length drive off on the volley, or he will turn the tables, putting the pressure on you.

The straight shot must be kept tight to the side wall, so restricting your opponent's choice of reply. A ball 'glued' to the side wall is a very difficult one to return, especially if it has pace on it. Any shot your opponent makes inevitably comes away from the wall, giving you the opportunity to continue the attack. The better the standard of squash you play, the tighter you have to be, otherwise an eager opponent will benefit from your loose width. The safest length shot is the straight shot, as the width is easier to control and less likely to be cut off by an eager opponent.

Only play the cross-court shot when you are sure that you can

Length

Width

Rodney Martin (Australia), one of the most exciting players in world squash today. (Photograph: Stephen Line)

pass your opponent. Any such shot with poor width can easily be cut off on the volley, so putting you under a great deal of pressure. With your cross-court shots, aim to play the ball so that it strikes the side wall around the back of the service box, so passing your opponent and forcing him to play his next shot out of the back corner. The width of any cross-court shot obviously depends on where your opponent is on the court, so be aware of his position when playing cross-court.

Control of the 'T' It is a very satisfying feeling to be in total control of the rally, directing operations from the centre of the court and watching your opponent running from corner to corner, frantically trying to retrieve your shot, gradually slowing to a crawl.

When playing the ball, always try to make sure that your opponent has to hit it out of one of the four corners of the court. This can really only be achieved by taking control of the 'T' area of the court. To stay in command, it is vital to volley the ball – you must hunt it in the air, not just volley when it comes to you. All the top players in the world, past and present, have been good volleyers, always making their opponent work harder than themselves. It is, of course, physically harder to take the ball early on the volley than it is to let it go and retrieve it from the back of the court, so you have to be fit to volley continually.

On the 'T', keep your racket head up. There is little chance of volleying the ball if it is dangling by your ankles. Be on the balls of your feet, racket up, watching the ball closely and ready to pounce on your opponent's shot. With experience, you will learn to watch his racket as well, gaining a valuable split second of reaction time to move into position to play a balanced shot.

Good length and width are the key to control of the 'T' area; having hit the ball to the back of the court, quickly take up position so that you are ready for your opponent's next shot early, exerting maximum pressure.

When playing the ball, select a shot that enables you to recover to the 'T' before your opponent plays the next shot. You should aim to be balanced, watching, before the next shot of the rally is played. By controlling the 'T' and taking the ball early, you are forcing your opponent to play his next shot under pressure. Imagine that, having played a length drive from a back corner, you are recovering to the 'T' area when your opponent cuts the ball off, sending you off in another direction to play it and forcing you to twist and turn, which is very tiring. This is what you must do to your opponent, imposing yourself forcefully on the game by gaining and keeping control of the centre of the court.

Game strategy

Early on in a match, length driving and volleying are of paramount importance. Keep your opponent buried in the 'graveyard' area of the court, letting him become used to his place there. In this part of the match don't send your opponent to the front of the court too soon, as he is still fresh and full of running, but first draw the life out of his legs. Extend these early rallies and make them hard.

Once you have pushed your opponent back with relentless length, begin to run him around the court. First of all, you have him deep; now work him short, then deep again, making him run the length of the court. Play the ball away from your opponent into the open court, keeping him on the move. An opponent at full stretch causes few problems: instead he will be content with just getting the ball back. Work him up and down the court, making him twist and turn as much as possible.

Having sent your opponent to the back of the court, it is important to look for the volley in order to keep up the pressure. Learn from Qamar Zaman, the wizard of Pakistan squash, who once said in a magazine article: 'A man who does not volley has only one reason for playing squash, that is to do a lot of running and lose weight.' It is also equally important, when your opponent is in a front corner, to look to volley any shot played to the back of the court. If you hang back when behind an opponent, he is far more likely to get away with any shot he plays to the back. When you've sent him forward, move up to the 'T' area so that you can cut off the straight or cross-court shot. Don't let him back into the rally by allowing the ball to go to the back of the court. If by chance your opponent tries to catch you out with a short shot, you can also cover this. As always, keep up the pressure: very few people can cope with it if applied long enough.

The early driving, with pace, to a length (it is important that the ball goes all the way to the back and doesn't catch the side wall on the way) is the softening-up process, the foundation of the match on which to build. Remember, though, that it is no good just hitting the ball aimlessly in the general direction of the back corners. You must make every shot work for you and against your opponent, keeping him on the stretch and never allowing him to settle. This should begin to force the errors out of him as he starts to show the first signs of oxygen debt and begins to slow. The first round of the battle has now been won and you can push home your superiority as the loose replies appear, giving you the chance to go for winners. If you are unable to put away the first chance, don't panic: work patiently for your opening again.

When and how do you send your opponent to the front of the court? First, if he is balanced, ready, and in position, don't; work him deep, out of position. When you have got him moving, hurrying to regain control, use the drop and the boast to work him forward. If an opponent is used to you playing a length shot from behind him, suddenly put in a two-wall boast, drawing him right forward. Remember to move up to cover the reply, cutting it off on the volley if possible, so keeping your opponent moving faster than he wants to. The long drop off a loose shot is also an effective method of attack. Both shots help to break up your opponent's rhythm, preventing him from settling and starting to think about making you work.

Making it as physically hard as possible for your opponent in the

Jansher Khan (Pakistan) looking to take the ball early on the volley to keep the pressure on his opponent. (Photograph: Stephen Line)

early stages of a match has already been discussed. Try also to extend the first game (always assuming you are fit enough!). Keep it simple, selecting your shots with care. Think about playing the basic shot from any position to begin with, you can always develop your game as the match progresses and you become more confident against a tiring opponent.

Attempt winners when you are balanced, having worked for your opportunity and when sure you can recover to the 'T' area and so

Jahangir Khan (Pakistan) playing a backhand drop with Del Harris (England) out of position. (Photograph: Stephen Line)

cover your opponent's next shot. If you choose the right moment to play the winner, you should have more time. This applies particularly when playing a drop shot from the front half of the court. The deeper your opponent is buried, the more out of position he is, the less the pressure on you. Remember that your drop is going to be only as good as the quality of your length and don't play it too soon.

In squash, as you can score points only when serving, it is important to make the most of this opportunity. However, if by some chance you do make an error, at least you don't give away a point, only the service. This is bad enough, but still your opponent doesn't get a point. The same does not apply when you are hand-out: any error then costs a point and your opponent needs to score only 9 to win a game.

When you are hand-in, you can afford to go for your shots more often. Still, work for your openings – don't try to be clever, going for them at the wrong time when your opponent is balanced and ready to pounce at the slightest opportunity. This doesn't apply so much when you are hand-out; then you cannot afford to hit the tin or put the ball out of court. Work more cautiously for your openings; don't become totally negative, but choose your moment to go for the winners far more carefully.

If in your matches you can cut out the unforced errors, this will make a tremendous difference to your game. You need not worry that you will become totally negative; you are just being more patient, and will still have plenty of opportunities to play your shots. The secret is to learn the right moment to go for them and, in this way, the unforced errors should start to disappear and you will become a far harder opponent to beat. It is the unforced errors that cost matches, so work hard to cut these 'gifts' out of your game. There are always going to be times when you make an error, but don't give your opponent the rally – make him work for it and really make him force a mistake out of you.

Cutting the errors out of your game does not mean that you stop attacking; far from it. Keep the pressure on your opponent, but do so by giving yourself a little more margin for error with your drives, volleys, boasts and drops, especially when hand-out. Remember at all times to be as positive as the situation allows, and never let your opponent relax and settle. Once he knows what is coming all the time, there is no pressure, and he can concentrate on attacking you.

The defensive game

If you are on the receiving end, under pressure from an opponent putting a lot of pace on the ball and taking it early, how should you cope? You have to do two things: first, change the pace of the game; and second, stop your opponent taking the ball early on the volley. Unless you are very sure that you can out-hit your opponent, there is little sense in trying to do this. A hard hitter will feed off your pace and return it with interest, and there is a tendency to lose accuracy with your shots, hitting without purpose.

The front wall on a squash court is 15 feet (4.57m) high, so why try to use only the bottom 2–3 inches above the tin? When under pressure, use the full height on the front wall to slow the pace of the game, floating the ball up into the air, either down the side walls or cross-court. This type of tactical game requires a great deal of accuracy, otherwise an eager opponent will continue to cut the ball off on the volley. The width of any floated lob is very important;

straight shots must be glued to the side wall, and cross-court shots given plenty of width, catching the side wall around the back of the service box just below the out-of-court line. With both the straight and cross-court lobs, aim to drop the ball into the 'graveyard' area.

Height and width used well are a very effective way of breaking up the rhythm of an opponent who likes a fast, hard-hitting game. It is very difficult to impart any pace to a ball high up in the air, especially over the backhand side of the court. The effect of changing the pace of the game by lobbing an opponent can be devastating, turning a losing situation into a winning one, changing defence into attack. This defensive tactic, if applied well, gives you the chance to feed off any loose shots from your opponent, letting you inject pace when you want to, and turning the tables on him. When forced away from the 'T' at full stretch to return the ball, resist the temptation to try the clever shot. It is at this moment that self-discipline is so important: instead of trying to pull off the lucky winner, make your first priority to get the ball into a back corner. Whether at the front of the court, or in a back corner, use the full height on the front wall and the width of the court to lob the ball over your opponent's head. This shot gives you time to recover to the 'T' and, if played accurately enough, may force him to play the ball out of a back corner, giving you a chance to attack.

Variation of pace
Many good club and even county players show very little or no variation in the pace of their game. Generally they hit the ball hard and low; their game is one-paced. It is important, however, to develop the ability to be able to slow the game down, or speed it up, depending on the circumstances of the match, the physical condition of your opponent and of yourself. Pace variation is an art. Develop it during practice matches, gain confidence in your own ability and you will find that this pays dividends in your matches.

Many times in matches, the rallies are fast and furious, then one player hits a softer shot, so his opponent follows. Don't let your opponent dictate the tactics: you must work to impose *yourself* on the match. If you follow his pace, you are playing into your opponent's hands, making his life much easier. If you let your opponent play the game his way, his confidence rises, making it very difficult for you to break his stranglehold on the match.

You don't necessarily have to hit the ball harder to speed up the pace of the game. This can be done by taking the ball early. By volleying the ball, your opponent is going to have to work harder to stay in the rallies. Equally, slowing the pace down doesn't mean using the lob all the time. Instead of hitting your drives at full or three-quarter pace, put in a softer drive, at perhaps half-pace, which can be very disconcerting, upsetting the rhythm of your opponent.

Remember that, unless you are completely out-hitting your opponent, you should always try to vary the pace of a game. The distance runner who keeps running along at the same pace is very easy to follow; the runner though who puts in a fast lap, then settles again, then kicks again, is a difficult person to beat.

Strengths and weaknesses

Unless you are unusual, you will have some weakness in your game. Everybody likes practising their strength, but this is generally not the area of your game that is going to let you down. In practice, work to eradicate your weaknesses, to bring them up to near the level of your strength. It is very demoralizing to knock up with an opponent and play the first few points and not be able to pick out any weakness. So, if you do have a weakness, hide it by playing to your strength and don't give an opponent a chance to attack your Achilles' heel. Build your game around your strength and attack your opponent's weakness. Make him feel uncomfortable; get to him psychologically by not letting him settle to the task and keep probing his Achilles' heel, increasing the pressure until he cracks.

Once you have found that a particular tactic is paying dividends against an opponent, don't change a winning game. If an opponent cannot deal with your lob service and this is opening up the rally, giving you the opportunity to take command, then continue with it. If you slip in a harder, lower serve, this may be just the chance for your opponent to seize upon and could be the turning point in a match. He wins the rally, gains confidence and, with serve, looks a different player. This is an extreme example, but often matches do turn on a couple of rallies. You have shown a chink in your concentration, shown that you have mentally relaxed, giving your opponent an opening to attack.

Don't relax: the time for compassion is after the match. Remember that no match is yours until you've won three games. Total concentration is required to be a top squash player, a quality that only the true champions have. Jonah Barrington, Geoff Hunt and Jahangir Khan are good examples of players with this type of concentration.

On the other hand, if the game is beginning to slip away from you, be positive in your mental attitude. The negative approach is to sit back and hope that your opponent's good fortune cannot last. The positive approach is to change your game, giving your opponent something new and different to think about. It is important not to be panicked into changing your game. If the reason that you are losing is that your attempted drop winners are going into the tin, the solution is to cut out these shots. This is not such a wholesale change, just a sensible course of action to take. For a while, work on hitting the ball deep, concentrating on length and width, until your rhythm and confidence return, then reintroduce your short game.

At club level, many players seem blind to their opponent's strengths, continuing to feed their favourite shot. In the knock-up, and before any match, you should find out as much as possible about your opponent. (See page 77 for more about match preparation.) If he has a particular strength, starve that strength just as you would try to exploit a weakness; don't let him use his favourite shot. This will certainly get to your opponent and, eventually, he will try to play this shot off a ball that is not quite there and make an error.

Quite often left-handers cause right-handed players problems, because the right-handers don't know how to play against them. There are far more right-handed players, so they don't get much practice against left-handers. If you find yourself faced with a left-handed opponent, keep a cool head: he is not superhuman. You simply have to readjust your thinking, remembering to serve from the left, to your opponent's backhand. There is nothing more unsettling than to put the ball on to an opponent's racket in the first serve of the match and see it disappear away for a winner.

Many left-handers, at club level, have a weaker backhand than forehand, struggling especially with the ball high on their backhand. Try deliberately keeping the ball away from their more powerful forehand and keep working at their backhand, slowly eating away at their confidence. You can even serve down the middle rather than to their forehand. I don't guarantee the tactic will work against every left-hander, but try it and, if there is no success, change tactics. Above all, don't be overawed by playing a left-hander: concentrate on the job in hand, patiently working for your openings.

Patience is very important in squash. How often do you see a player going for an early winner off the half-chance and making an error, letting his opponent in? Through having confidence in your own ability, your patience to wait and probe for the opening to go for a winner will increase. If your opponent returns your shot, you won't panic, but will patiently work for the opportunity once more to attempt to go for a winner. If you are confident in your racket work and fitness, you can relax more and be patient. This can be very disturbing for your opponent, who begins to wonder if he is ever going to make any impression on your game. By being patient, you can rally with your opponent, waiting till the right moment when you

Chris Dittmar (Australia)
moving in for the kill.
(Photograph: Stephen Line)

are balanced and he is right out of position to go for a winner. Everything comes to he who waits.

Try to develop an armoury of shots from a particular position in the court, so that you can keep your opponent guessing. This is not

69

to say that you should always play a different shot from the same position: the shot you hit depends on where your opponent is, whether you are balanced, and the state of the match. Do try not to rely on your favourite shot to win matches, as you will attempt it when the ball is not really there for it and make unforced errors. A player who has to rely on a 'pet' shot is a very limited player indeed. Remember: build your shots around a sound basic game. Any variation or 'wrong-footing' shot is only as good as the basic shot from that position. Show your opponent the straight drive; then, after a number of straight shots from that position, he becomes conditioned to it. That is the time to slip in the cross-court shot. (See page 56 for more about deception.)

In squash, there is nothing more disconcerting than the player who keeps getting your best shots back again. The long-term effect is that this eats away at your confidence, as you try to go tighter and tighter with your winners, cutting down your margin of error, and then you start hitting the tin. The point to be made from this is: never give up; no ball is a lost cause. If you run for everything, it is surprising what you can pick up – even if you just pop it up over the tin, at least your opponent has to play another shot. It can be very frustrating for him if you keep retrieving the seemingly hopeless, and quite often the end result is that your opponent puts the ball into the tin. So develop the 'never say die' attitude, and always refuse to accept that the cause is lost.

As you are well aware, a squash court has a number of lines on the floor. Try looking at these afresh and add a few imaginary lines as well, to help your game. You can even try actually marking them on the court with tape during practice, so that they have become imprinted on your mind by the time you come to play in a match, and you will see how your game has improved.

If the edges of the service box on both sides of the court are extended (see the illustration) to the front and back wall, they produce two long, narrow corridors. In squash, every shot should bounce in one or other of these channels. Discipline yourself to keep the ball away from the middle wider rectangle, as any ball passing through this area can easily be cut off by your opponent. The higher the level of squash you play, the narrower these channels need to be - say, half the service box width or less.

Keeping the ball away from the centre of the court makes life harder for your opponent, but unless you also concentrate on where your shots bounce in the corridors, it will not take them far enough away from the 'T' to cause too many problems. Try adding some more imaginary lines to the court. Aim your length drives, volleys

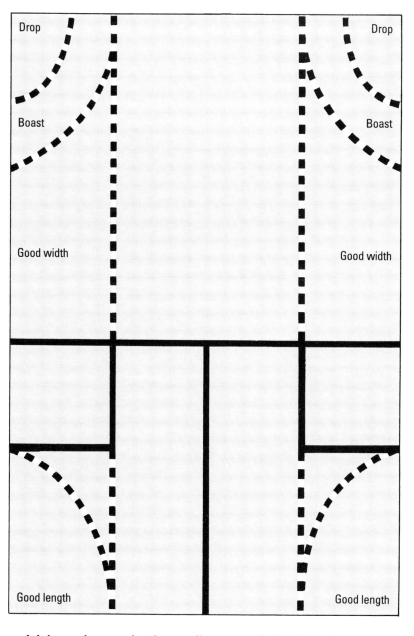

Drop

Drop

Boast

Boast

Good width

Good width

Good length

Good length

Map of the court floor identifying targets to aid development of a tighter game.

and lobs to bounce in the smaller target behind the back of the service box, ensuring that your opponent has to go right into the back corner away from the centre of the court, giving you command of the 'T' area.

In the front corners of the court, there are two target areas, one for the boasts and kills, the other for drop shots. For the boasts and kills, imagine an area similar in size to the rectangle behind the back of the service box. Aim your boasts to bounce in this area, so taking your opponent right to the front of the court. The target for the drops needs to be smaller in size (see the illustration), so keeping the ball even tighter to the front corner.

The area on either side of the court, between the two targets, is no man's land, like the middle. Any ball landing in there is neither one thing nor the other, neither short nor long, and therefore puts little pressure on your opponent. There are good shots that do not land in the target areas, especially when cutting the ball across your opponent's body. However, by and large, if you concentrate on keeping the ball out of the middle of the court and bouncing in either the front or back targets, life will be much harder for your opponent.

The boast in squash is a shot that often causes problems, especially when played at the wrong moment with an eager opponent watching on the 'T', ready to pounce. Remember that, through good-quality length and width, you are trying to force your opponent to boast. This sets you up with an easy ball at the front of the court to apply more pressure, with your opponent out of position.

Ideally, use the boast only when you want to; don't be forced into using it unless it is as a last resort and the only way you can return the ball. However, many players boast when – if they stayed out of the back corner and just reached in with the racket, getting the racket head behind the ball – they could straighten it. You will find that, if you practise, eventually you will be able to straighten a lot of balls you used to boast.

Use the two-wall boast to break up the rhythm of the rally, to move your opponent forward, drawing him into a front corner. This can be especially effective against a player who takes his eye off you as you play your shot, or who hangs back, expecting a length shot. However, don't overuse this shot, especially early in a match when your opponent is fresh, with lots of running in his legs. As the match progresses, the boast can be a very effective way of tiring an opponent. If you know your opponent is slow to the front of the court, in this case the boast can be an effective weapon even early on in a match.

If your opponent is using the boast, how do you deal with it? If you can quickly pounce on the ball, trying to get on to it early, before it strikes the third wall, then play a drop shot. It can be very effective, if you reach the ball early, to cut it across your body, not aiming at the nick but wide enough to make it difficult for your opponent to return, forcing him to twist and turn to retrieve it. Play this shot early, with plenty of cut, so that it doesn't sit up – you will find that quite often it dies by the short line. Ideally, aim for the second bounce to be near the opposite side wall. This is a shot used to great effect by the Pakistanis. Try it: surprise your opponents.

On the other hand, if you don't reach the ball early, drive it deep into the 'graveyard' areas of the court, straight and tight to the side. If really stretched, use the height on the front wall, lob high and wide across the court, or down the wall. Either way, make sure your opponent cannot cut the ball off on the volley.

The boast can be a very effective weapon, but use it sparingly. Boast when *you* want to, not when forced to do so. Learn to avoid boasting under pressure; instead, get your racket head behind the ball and straighten it.

Here is a check-list to help you with your game.

Summary

1. Develop a sound basic game, based on good-quality length and width.
2. Control the 'T' area by looking to hunt the ball in the air, volleying it at every opportunity.
3. Watch the ball at all times, especially when it is behind you, keeping the racket up while waiting to pounce.
4. Serve well. Don't waste this chance to put your opponent under maximum pressure.
5. Return service safely. Move the server away from the 'T' into a back corner to take control of the centre of the court.
6. Vary the pace of the game, using height and width. Don't be a one-paced player.
7. When under pressure, use the lob with plenty of height and width to give yourself time to recover to the 'T' area.
8. Make your opponent run by playing the ball away from him, moving him up and down the court.
9. Don't send your opponent to the front of the court too early in a match when he is fresh, with lots of running in his legs.
10. Develop a patient approach. Wait until you have worked your opponent out of position and you are balanced before going for a winner.
11. Look to play your winners from the front half of the court.
12. Early on in the match, make it physically hard for your opponent. Play a pressurized basic game to take an early lead.

13. Play to your strengths, eradicate weaknesses in your own game, and attack your opponent's weaknesses.
14. Cut out the unforced errors from your game.
15. Chase everything, be positive in your approach. Remember that nothing is a lost cause.
16. Remember that your drop is only as good as the quality of your length and your variation shots are only as good as your basic game.
17. Above all, develop the ability to play a tight, attacking game, choosing the right moment to go for your shots.
18. Finally, remember it is impossible to play badly if you do the basics well.

Tournament preparation and play

3

As the season draws near and the first tournaments are not very far away, the moment of truth is fast approaching when you will see if all your background training during the summer is going to pay off. Now is the time to be 'fining down', concentrating on speed work to build on the endurance work done in the middle of summer.

Imagine that your first tournament or important match is a month away. Certainly by now, all the heavy endurance training should have been completed. The emphasis at this point, to bring yourself to match fitness, should be plenty of hard games, speed work and racket work. The combination of these three elements should help you to 'peak' for the tournament – that is, arriving physically and mentally fit, sharp from the hard matches and racket work you have done. Do not allow the phrase 'he left it all on the training ground' apply to you; do not train so that you reach the event jaded and unable to perform to the best of your ability.

Geoff Hunt and Jonah Barrington were past masters at preparing themselves well for an event, so that they arrived physically and mentally fresh for the battles ahead. During Hunt's last two years in competitive squash, before he was forced to retire because of injury, he would often be beaten in tournaments leading up to the British Open. However, when this event arrived, he was in superb condition, while his opponents couldn't understand how, after they had beaten him only weeks before, he now appeared invincible. The secret lay in his careful build-up, planned meticulously, so that he peaked at precisely the right time.

It is an art developed, not only through very careful timetabling of your training build-up, but also through personal experience. Naturally, the way in which a player prepares for a tournament depends very much on how he individually reacts to training. The final month before the big event is critical and can only be worked out by listening to advice from your coach and drawing on your own past experience. This is why keeping a training diary – referred to in the chapter on training (see page 93) – is so important. By looking back through it you can see what you did while preparing, how you reacted and how you performed during the actual tournament. This four-week build-up before a big event should help gradually to 'fine down' the hard physical (endurance) training and increase the speed element through ghosting. In the two weeks leading up to the tournament, there should be little or no training off court, but rather you should concentrate on using the racket to work on your shots and in playing matches. In this way, you come to a peak of match fitness. The last week should be easy, with the emphasis again on racket work.

However, what are you going to do if unable to devote so much time to preparation because you have to work for a living and time is limited? The answer is to concentrate on playing and practising, rather than on training. As long as you have a sound background of endurance work, you can use hard matches to sharpen up your game. Even though you have little time, try to set aside fifteen or twenty minutes every day to keep the stretching going regularly. This is very important if injuries are to be prevented – the more so, the older you are.

Assuming your build-up to the first tournament of the season has gone well and you're now into the last week, with the tournament starting on Friday, the worst thing you can do is to have a physically hard week. The net result of this will be for you to arrive feeling jaded and so perform below par. It is important to concentrate on racket work, with certainly no hard games after the Monday of that week, so that you have three easy days before the first round.

If the first day of an event is a working day for you, it is difficult to arrive early enough to allow sufficient time between getting out of the car and stepping on to the court. Ideally, take a day's holiday and travel the previous day, or at least during the Friday morning, so that you arrive by lunchtime or early afternoon. This gives you enough time to eat a meal, relax and perhaps have a hit on the courts where you are going to play, so that you get a feel for their pace and can check the height, walls, lighting and the floor. Even if it is not possible to go on court, try to watch somebody else there, or at least have a good look at the court to see what type it is. Check what the floor is like; is it sealed? How dark are the walls? What is the plaster like? How large are the nicks? How high is the roof of the court and what colour is it? What are the lighting arrangements? Does the court have a glass back wall? If so, is there a white board behind it? If not, the back corners tend to be very dark, making it difficult to see the ball when it is in the 'graveyard' area.

Finally, how warm are the courts? This will have a bearing on your approach to the game. Very cold courts make a retrieving game much harder to play, as the ball tends to die more quickly, so favouring a 'shot' player rather than one who prefers to rely on his fitness, rallying to keep the ball going and forcing the errors out of his opponent. Conversely, warm courts favour the retriever, as it is harder to kill a lively ball which tends to sit up, unless you hit it very accurately. This is why it is useful to develop a solid all-round game, so that you are able to adapt to different court conditions.

At the beginning and end of the season, there is often a considerable temperature change from day to night, and unless courts are well ventilated there may be a danger of condensation, which makes playing very difficult as the ball reacts totally differently off a wet surface. If you are unfortunate to be playing on a court that starts sweating, cut out any boast shots or lobs and concentrate on hitting the ball hard and low. This is very effective under such conditions, because the ball picks up moisture off the walls and, when it bounces, tends to skid, not reacting as one would expect. Lobs, when they strike the front wall, tend to carry on upwards into the roof; and with boasts the ball doesn't grip the side wall but skids and so ends up in the middle of the court.

In advance of the tournament, find out the match scheduling so that you know how many games you will have to play over the weekend if you are lucky enough to reach the final. This should ensure that you are not caught out, having to go on to court unprepared. Discover what type of ball is being used, as different types react differently, and try to practise with it prior to the tournament.

Once you receive the draw, and you know whom you are playing, find out as much about your opponent as possible. Talk to people who have played him, to discover his strengths and weaknesses, so that you can work out your strategy. Attacking your opponent's weaknesses and starving his strengths has already been discussed (see page 67); if you are unable to find out anything before arriving at the tournament, talk to other players from your opponent's area of the country. Avoid going on to court not knowing anything about him.

In the week leading up to the tournament, try to keep your usual routine. Any dramatic change can upset your natural body rhythms, affecting the way you perform on court. Going to bed early if you are not accustomed to doing so is probably not going to help; it is of paramount importance to stay relaxed and changing your sleeping pattern may have an adverse effect. It is, however, helpful to increase the body's carbohydrate intake, to build up the glycogen stores in the muscles and liver (see page 91). Over the weekend of the tournament, eating regularly will often be difficult because food has to be fitted in around match times, making it awkward to eat a large meal during the day.

When the time comes to prepare to leave for the tournament, remember to give yourself plenty of time to pack. There is nothing worse than arriving at the club to find you've left something behind. If possible, take with you enough clothing to allow yourself a fresh set of kit for every round. It is unpleasant having to put on damp socks, shorts and shirt – and your opponent will appreciate this as well.

In addition to your squash clothing, make sure that you have checked your rackets. Don't leave for a tournament with the strings of your favourite racket about to break or needing new grips. Have two rackets that are the same as regards weight, balance and handle size, so that if one breaks you are not thrown by having to use another with a different feel in the middle of a match. Professional tennis players have three or four rackets in case of emergency. While I am not suggesting that you go to that extreme, certainly have two rackets the same. If you use a towelling grip on your racket, put new grips on before leaving: don't wait until five minutes before going on to court. The new gauze or 'Tourna' grips need changing frequently.

Your squash bag should contain the following: spare grips; a small first-aid kit; a bag for your squash shoes and one for your damp kit; soap and shampoo (make sure the top is firmly on – you do not want a shampoo-covered squash kit!); a stiff brush to rough up your racket grips if you use towelling ones; a hairbrush or comb; two towels – one for use during the matches and one to use for showering afterwards – a resin pad if you use it; and a small stringing kit for repairing any broken strings.

It might appear that you will need a very large squash bag to carry all this, but it is better to be well prepared for nearly every eventuality than have to rush around between matches trying to find some item which you have failed to bring when you should be relaxing. The stringing kit need be only a pair of small wire cutters, two awls, an old racket handle and a length of gut or synthetic stringing, depending on what you use. If it is gut, remember to take it out of your bag after the weekend, and keep it away from damp kit when in the bag. A small first-aid kit is really essential and need only include butterfly plasters, fabric sticking plasters (a box of assorted sizes or, if in strip form, ready cut for use), Spenco second skin, Hirudoid cream, sterile dressings with bandage (especially eye-patch dressings), 1·5cm stretch tape (for blisters) small pack, Tubigrip (knee or ankle size) and scissors.

Pain-relieving spray has not been included in the first-aid kit as it is not to be recommended for the reason that it can give an athlete a false impression of the severity of any injury. Pain is the body's warning system that something is wrong: deaden it, continue playing and you could be causing further damage which may keep you out of action for longer than would have been necessary. Pay attention to the warning signs from your body.

The case of a very talented junior player underlines this advice. At the beginning of the season in September, he had beaten the number one seed in the semi-final of his first under-nineteen tournament. Towards the end of this match, he felt as though he had slightly strained a hamstring. In the period between the semi-final and the final, the muscle stiffened up considerably, so he very carefully stretched the hamstring before going on to play. He comfortably won the first two games, but the leg was now quite sore, so he applied a pain-relieving spray. Eventually he won 10-8 in the fifth. However, he did not really play competitive squash again until January the following year as a result of damaging further an already injured hamstring. This is rather an extreme example, but the message is clear: heed the warning signs – there is always tomorrow.

If you do turn an ankle over, pull a muscle or receive a blow with the racket during a match, use ice to reduce the swelling (caused by fluid), and use it immediately. Don't apply heat to the injury because this increases the swelling. Follow this simple formula: place ice on the injured area, taking care, if applying it directly to the skin, not to cause ice burns, then support the damaged limb. In the case of any injury, seek medical advice as soon as possible. An injury left untreated may become chronic and therefore harder to cure in the long run. Treatment within twenty-four hours is vital for a speedy recovery. Consult your doctor to find out where the nearest sports injury clinic is.

If you are struck in the eye by a ball, always seek medical advice quickly, even if the blow didn't appear to be a bad one. It is far better to have your eye checked immediately than to suffer damage to your vision for the rest of your life. If you wear glasses while playing, make sure the lenses are plastic; if you wear contact lenses, they should be soft ones. While on the subject of glasses, here are two tips from a fellow sufferer for preventing them misting up. One idea given to me by Philip Ayton, former Great Britain international, is to wash the lenses in cold water to remove all dirt and grease, then dry them with a soft tissue. Keep clean tissues available to wipe your glasses between games, but try to avoid keeping them off for too long, as it is change in temperature which causes the misting effect. Another way to combat misting is with a Calotherm spray, available from opticians. Apply this to both sides of the lenses, having cleaned them first, then wipe dry. This provides a protective film, so even if you have to wipe them between games, they should not mist up. It is also a good idea to wear a towelling headband to prevent sweat from dropping on to the lenses. Unfortunately the rules of squash do not allow time to clean glasses in-between rallies; play must be continuous, so it pays to take time to clean them carefully before you start.

The match All the pre-tournament preparations are now complete and you are within the final hour before your match. Ideally, you should plan your warm-up to finish almost immediately before you go on to court. It is a good idea not to wear your match kit for the warm-up or it will become damp before the start of the match. Instead, wear an old tracksuit, then towel down afterwards before putting on fresh kit and another tracksuit to keep you warm before going on to court for the knock-up (see page 82). This is what Jonah Barrington does so that he has fresh, dry kit for his match. The racket grips are brushed up, and in his bag – which he takes to the court side – are a towel, the brush, sticking plasters and a clean shirt. Psychologically, when you are feeling tired, the new shirt can give you a vital lift. Prior to the knock-up, get the spare shirt ready for a quick change – you do not want to be fumbling with buttons during the interval between games. Lastly, prepare a drink for in-between games.

Your match plan should be formulated, but be prepared to be adaptable as the match progresses if the game is not going your way. It is very encouraging to know somebody is there to help you between games, if only to have your drink and towel ready, whether you are the world champion or the club number one playing in the club tournament. Should you be helping a friend in this way, try not to give too much advice as very little can be taken in at this stage. An over-complicated game plan may only confuse. Keep the advice simple, combined with lots of positive encouragement. The last thing anybody needs, when coming off court having lost a game, is to have his confidence undermined.

After your match, the temptation is to head for the bar to get a drink and, before you know it, you have cooled off and stiffened up. Try to get into the habit of making straight for the changing room and warming down, stretching out the hamstrings, quadriceps, calves, adductors, shoulder and forearm. This helps to prevent stiffness following a hard game. Then take a shower and change into warm clothing. Following this, find out when your next match is, buy your opponent a drink and make arrangements to have something to eat. In between matches, it is often difficult to eat a large meal, but at least try to eat some easily digestible food with a high

carbohydrate content, to help replenish your depleted energy stores. It is not unusual, following a very hard match, to be unable to eat immediately, especially if you have just drunk a couple of pints of fluid.

Ross Norman (New Zealand) under pressure. (Photograph: Stephen Line)

81

At the end of the day, always try to ensure that you sit down to a good meal. Remember the saying: 'An army marches on its stomach' – squash players are very much the same. Have a proper meal and then return to your accommodation for a good night's sleep. Sometimes it is useful to have a book to read to help you relax and sleep more easily.

During a tournament, squash clubs can become very claustrophobic. You can waste a lot of nervous energy hanging around, waiting for the next round. To avoid this, try to get out of the club into the fresh air or, if possible, back to where you are staying. This will help you to relax and perhaps even have a short sleep. The important thing is to get away from the club, to give yourself a break, so you come back refreshed for the next match. Juniors tend to find it difficult to relax between rounds and instead of conserving their energy they are back playing on the first court available. Although this may not take very much out of them, it can mean the difference between winning and losing in the semi-final or final.

While on the subject of energy conservation, avoid the temptation during the early rounds to take things easy, dropping games because you are playing against weaker opposition. This is counter-productive; the best way to save yourself for later rounds is to get on and off the court as quickly as possible. Dropping unnecessary points, or an entire game, is quite often attributable to loss of concentration. Right from the moment you go on to court for your first match, shut out everything but the match you are playing. It is no good thinking that you will suddenly be able to concentrate fully when under pressure in later rounds. Develop what is called 'tunnel vision' from the beginning of your first match.

The knock-up

By the time you step on to court, you should have warmed up well and be ready for the 'battle' ahead. The knock-up is not just to warm the ball up; it is your opportunity to groove your swing, so that when the first rally starts, you are timing the ball.

Begin by concentrating on hitting the ball at half-pace to a length with a good width, making sure you hit through it to find the rhythm to your swing. Don't try to hit the ball as hard as possible, risking injury. Use this opportunity to find out as much as you can about your opponent. Feed him for particular shots – a few lobs, boasts and volleys – to find out how he copes with them. Learn from what your opponent does and store this information away, along with any other you have, to use when the match starts. If he appears to be 'suspect' overhead, attack this area. If he doesn't

Jansher Khan (Pakistan), racket up, eye on the ball, moving forward to attack it. (Photograph: Stephen Line)

volley, your task will be so much easier. If he appears to be slow to the front of the court, as the match progresses exploit this.

At the same time, start hitting the ball from around the back of the service box, gradually moving up to take it from the short line on the volley. Take a few balls off the back wall, so that you are aware of how the ball rebounds off the wall. Play one or two boasts and get the feel of playing the ball from the back. Hopefully, you won't have to play many shots from there, but it is asking for trouble if the first time you do is in the first rally and you have not prepared yourself. Play a few shots from the front corners straight and cross-court to find your length. When assessing your opponent, hit a few balls very wide on to the side wall, to see how he copes with them: often even good volleyers struggle with the ball coming at them off the side wall.

When I first had some coaching, I was told that there were two schools of thought regarding the knock-up. According to the first, you should play as many shots as possible, retrieving everything your opponent throws at you, and so demoralizing him, giving him the impression that you can retrieve everything and you have a wide range of shots. The second school advocates that you fail to return everything, or that when you do you should hit it into the tin, lulling your opponent into a false sense of security, so he thinks all he has to do is keep the ball in play and he will win. Then, when the match starts, you should attack, catching your opponent off guard, and establish an early lead, so demoralizing him. Probably the best approach is somewhere between the two schools of thought, though personal experience has shown that at least one of them might have some value. In a club match, I went on to court with an opponent who started by hitting everything at one hundred miles an hour, aiming mainly at the nick. I returned hardly anything because I could barely see the ball, and when I did it was off the wood. However, I won the first game 9-0, playing tight length and width, and eventually won in the fifth. I had not planned to miss-hit everything in the knock-up, but perhaps occasionally it works!

In the knock-up you have five minutes to groove your swing, find out what you can about your opponent and to get the feel of the court. Don't stand in one spot; make sure you have played shots from all four corners of the court.

From the moment the marker calls love all, you should be totally prepared for the match, having left nothing to chance. You've covered everything, so if by some remote possibility you lose, it is because your opponent played better, not because your preparation let you down.

Fitness training

4

Many people play squash to lose weight and get fit, but this is really doing things the wrong way round. You need to be fit to play squash. The level of squash to which you aspire determines the fitness level you require. There is no doubt that the fitter you are, the easier the game becomes. The quicker you reach the ball, the more time you have to hit it, so you are under less pressure, able to dictate the pattern of the game.

There are five elements which make up the complete squash player: technique, tactics, psychology, health and fitness.

It is important to remember, when talking about fitness, not to lose sight of the fact that it is only one of the five components that go together to make a good squash player. If you concentrate on one item on the list to the detriment of the others you are not going to be a complete player.

Physical fitness increases the efficiency of the different parts of the body used in a particular sport. As it is achieved, certain bodily changes occur.

The lungs

The function of the lungs is both to pass oxygen from the air to the red blood cells and to disperse carbon dioxide from the blood. (The blood carries the oxygen to the muscles, which require it for exercise, and brings away the carbon dioxide, one of the waste products created.) After a period of training, there may be a small increase in the capacity of the lungs, but they are not very 'trainable' under normal conditions. Smokers can experience the problem of breathlessness more readily than non-smokers during any form of exercise, and the effectiveness of the lungs is particularly reduced for an hour or so after each cigarette.

The exchange of gases in the lungs occurs in millions of tiny air sacs. If it were possible to lay all these out flat, they would cover an area the size of a squash-court floor. At rest, you are probably breathing in and out each minute about 6 to 8 litres of air from which $\frac{1}{3}$ litre of oxygen is absorbed. However, while exercising during a hard squash match, this amount can increase by fifteen times, so that 100 litres are breathed in and out, of which 4 litres are oxygen which will be absorbed.

The amount of oxygen available to the working muscles in the body is determined by the rate at which the heart can pump blood around the body, not on the size of the lungs. The body has only a small oxygen store, just enough for about twenty seconds of exercise. Therefore you need to stimulate the brain to increase your oxygen intake. The way to do this is to cause the muscles to produce carbon dioxide, a waste product of exercise. The carbon dioxide in the blood stimulates the respiratory centre in the brain to increase the rate of breathing – another good reason for warming up well before a match.

Despite its small capacity for storing oxygen, the body can – for about forty seconds – undertake a major physical effort without breathing in extra air. The reason is that the body is capable of producing energy without oxygen (see page 89), but with a penalty. Usually this occurs in the first five minutes of a game, so the body needs to absorb extra oxygen, enough to cover the work being done and also to pay back the oxygen debt incurred before the breathing rate 'catches up' with the rate of exercise. Once this balance has been restored, and the oxygen absorbed satisfies the requirements, the body is in a 'steady state', more commonly known as 'second wind'. How often do you feel that the initial pace of a match is far too fast for you and that you'll never last the first game, yet as the game goes on it becomes easier? This is because you have got your 'second wind'.

The heart As the heart is a muscle, it can be increased in size through regular hard exercise over a period of months. Because both trained and untrained athletes produce roughly the same maximum heart rate, we know that training does not increase this rate, but it does increase the stroke volume (the amount of blood pumped out with each beat of the heart). The reason for this is that the trained athlete's heart becomes larger. The chambers of the heart increase in size and the muscular walls become stronger and thicker.

So the increase in heart rate and stroke volume enable the heart to pump more oxygen which carries the blood to the working muscles of the body. The amount of blood which the heart can pump is the main limiting factor in sports, requiring high degrees of cardio-respiratory fitness.

Training usually reduces the athlete's resting heart rate by between 20 and 30 per cent, which means that there is a greater range between the resting and maximum rates within which the heart works. At near-maximum rates (around 200 at the age of twenty, but decreasing with age) the heart cannot work efficiently, as its chambers cannot fill fast enough.

The red blood cells

During exercise, there may be a small increase in the number of red cells and therefore of oxygen-carrying haemoglobin in the blood, after an extended period of training (months rather than weeks). This is not, therefore, an important factor relating to fitness under normal conditions, though it may well be so for athletes competing at altitude where there is less oxygen in the air.

The circulatory system

During exercise, the body's circulatory system changes the pattern of blood flow (and therefore of oxygen supply) so that less travels to the organs not directly involved with exercise and more is provided to the working muscles. The required increase in oxygen is mainly supplied by the increased rate and depth of breathing and stroke volume of blood. However, extra oxygen comes as a result of blood being 'shunted' away from organs such as the liver, kidneys and digestive tract. The reason why it is dangerous to play sport on a full stomach (apart from a risk of 'stitch') is that it may put an extra load on the heart (fine if it is healthy, but not if it is diseased).

The muscle cells

There are a wide variety of changes which occur in exercised muscles. Some are concerned with aerobic training (see page 96), which is related to oxygen transportation and use. Greater delivery of blood to each muscle cell is assisted by an increase in the capillary blood vessels for a given area of muscle. There is also a large increase in the amount of myoglobin in each muscle cell with training, which can act as an oxygen store but more importantly transports oxygen within the muscle cell.

Myoglobin is the internal distributing agent in the muscle cell. It is the enzyme which uses oxygen chemically to release energy from the muscle fuel stores. This fuel is stored in mitochondria which, with training, not only increase in size and internal surface area, but also in number.

To summarize, training does have an effect on the working muscles. The cells of the muscles, unlike other cells in the body, can work effectively, albeit for short periods of time, without oxygen, i.e. anaerobically (see page 89). Muscles can be trained to work more efficiently.

Body cooling Heat is produced as a result of muscles releasing energy. Training increases the efficiency of the body's cooling system, and the body can regulate its temperature more effectively in the trained athlete. In men the main means of heat loss is sweating; in women radiation is the predominant means of heat loss. Sweating is a more effective method of regulating heat loss than radiation, unless the court is very humid, although too much fluid may be lost – and this should be replaced.

In the trained athlete, the temperature and heart rate do not rise as high as in the untrained person.

Body weight Body weight is an indirect factor in fitness. A reduction or even just redistribution in weight go hand in hand with becoming fitter. If an athlete's body weight does not drop during training, even though the percentage of body fat does, this is because muscle tissue has increased. Any weight loss, however, is due to a decrease in body fat. In squash, the less surplus weight a player has to carry the better, as the leg muscles and heart do not have to work as hard. For club players, the upper limit for body fat is 15 per cent for men and 28 per cent for women; for county players 12 per cent men and 26 per cent women; and for good internationals 10 per cent for men and 23 per cent for women. These figures are only guidelines, however.

Types of training What are the requirements that need to be trained for by the squash player?

Cardio-respiratory fitness, local muscle endurance, speed, strength, agility, flexibility, and a certain percentage of body fat.

Cardio-respiratory fitness Often called aerobic fitness – the ability of the heart, blood and lungs to transport adequate amounts of oxygen to the working muscles – this can be greatly improved through training. A simple method of checking whether you are responding to this type of training is to take the resting pulse rate in the morning, when you wake, to see if it is getting lower. Cardio-respiratory fitness is very important for squash.

Local muscle endurance This is the ability of a muscle, over a long period of time, to work without tiring. Squash requires a high degree of local muscle endurance in the legs, stomach, back, shoulder and racket arm.

There are two sides to muscle endurance: aerobic (working with oxygen) and anaerobic (working without oxygen). Both need to be trained.

Aerobic

In the muscles the capillaries transport the oxygenated blood to the myoglobin, which transfers it to the mitochondria, to mix it with the body's fuel to produce energy. As stated earlier, the capillaries, myoglobin and mitochondria can be increased considerably by training, making for a more efficient working system in the muscle.

Anaerobic

The muscles get their energy from the 'fuel' without oxygen. This method can generate more energy and power, but there is a penalty – lactic acid. When training or playing, if your limbs begin to feel heavy and you find it difficult to move quickly, the reason is a build-up of lactic acid.

The body can be trained to deal with lactic acid by means of a chemical 'buffer' system. Bicarbonate in the blood mops up the lactic acid, and the amount of bicarbonate can be increased through training. Lactic acid is also taken out of the blood by the liver, kidney and heart muscle, acted on by enzymes and then recycled back to glucose. This process increases with training.

Speed

In squash, speed is a very important element. The quicker you reach the ball, the more time you have to play your shot. All the greater players of the past, and Jahangir Khan today, are naturally quick, especially to the front of the court.

Speed has at least three components relevant to the squash player: decision time, reaction time and movement time (the time the working muscle takes to complete a movement). Muscle speed – the time taken by the muscle to contract – is a very important part of movement time and is related to the proportion of what are called 'fast' and 'slow' muscle cells. The sprinter will have a high proportion of fast muscle cells, the marathon runner more slow muscle cells. Fast cells can be trained, requiring a heavy workload for there to be any training effect.

Speed is very important in squash. Make sure your training programme has more than an element of speed work in it.

Strength

Squash does require a certain amount of body strength, but it is not a prime requirement for hitting a squash ball hard; co-ordination is far more important. However, a player should have adequate grip strength to prevent the racket turning in his hand if the ball is struck hard off-centre. This causes loss of accuracy, especially towards the end of a long match. A grip strength of 55 kilograms (men) or 45 kilograms (women) in the racket arm is satisfactory for county-standard players.

The legs, especially the thighs, also need strength to enable you to push off to the ball and recover after playing your shot. It is important to have a strong lower back too, because this area of the body takes a lot of pounding in squash.

Agility

This is something seen in all the great squash players, both men and women. They have the ability to move quickly without appearing to run around the court, gliding across the surface. It is something which is, by and large, innate and cannot specifically be trained, but practising and playing will develop your inherent agility.

Flexibility

Believe it or not, this is not a prime factor for squash, but it is important to prevent injury. Later the need to warm up properly before training and playing is stressed; stretching the muscle groups and mobilizing the joints is very important and should become part of your daily programme, even on your rest day!

Body fat

Remember that a low percentage of body fat is required in a squash player. Don't go on crash diets to bring yours down; exercise and a sensible diet will gradually lower it to an acceptable level (see below).

Nutrition

The human body can be likened to a car which cannot function without fuel. The energy expended by the body must be balanced by the food intake, otherwise the body utilizes its reserves of fat for fuel and weight is lost. The energy balance has a direct effect on an athlete's performance.

A squash player, like any human being, needs a balanced diet, but his food intake must be sufficient to meet the considerable requirements of the game. Squash is one of the highest energy-expending sports, so a player should aim for a high-carbohydrate diet. Depending on the sport played and the size of the individual, the body needs between 3000 and 8000 kilocalories per day. It naturally finds its own level of food intake, so excess fat is not put on with the greater number of kcals eaten. The size of the athlete and the workload determine the energy requirements, and so the food intake.

The food we eat can be broken down into the following components: carbohydrates, fats, protein, vitamins and minerals, all of which are essential to maintain good health. Carbohydrates are made up of sugars and starches and are the main source of energy in human diet. Rich sources include bread, potatoes, rice, pasta, sugar, honey, sweet fruits and milk. Fats also provide energy and energy reserves and are found in liquid form in oil, and in solid form from animal fats, butter and margarine. Protein is required to maintain healthy body tissue and, in the young, for growth, and is found in meat, fish, poultry, cheese, milk and eggs. In a well-balanced diet, vitamins are found naturally, so there is no real need to take any vitamin supplements. Minerals are present in milk, meat, vegetables and fruit.

The final vital ingredient of any diet is, of course, fluid. Sensible fluid intake is very important, as dehydration has a disastrous effect on physical performance. As the body sweats more, less fluid is available for cooling it down, so it tends to over-heat and performance deteriorates. While training and practising, get into the habit of taking some fluid before and during the exercise period, to replace that lost through sweating. Thirty minutes before exercise, drink 400–600 mls of water, then during exercise take 100–200 mls of water every fifteen minutes. When on court take a small drink between games. This can contain a weak glucose solution – no more than 4 per cent. Get into the habit of taking fluid during training so that your body adjusts to this: don't suddenly try it when playing an important match.

During exercise, there are extra demands on the body's fuel stores. The most readily available carbohydrate used as fuel is the glucose in the blood, which is absorbed from the intestine. Much of the carbohydrate not required immediately by the body is stored until needed as glycogen. There are two stores of glycogen in the body, one in the muscles and the other in the liver. During exercise, as the blood sugar supply is used and becomes inadequate, glycogen from the muscle tissue is used as fuel, being converted into glucose in the blood, so physical work can continue. The body's reserve of glycogen in the liver replaces the muscle glycogen as this is depleted by exercise.

The body's natural way of regulating its blood sugar level is by means of hormones, especially adrenalin and insulin. It is important to keep the blood sugar constant, as it is needed for brain activity as well as body movement. The brain has no store of its own it, so relies on the blood for its supply. This is why, if the blood sugar drops during exercise, you tend to lose concentration and co-ordination; as you tire physically, mental tiredness sets in as well, and you make more mistakes.

Regular meals are important for everybody, but particularly so for an athlete. Don't go all day without food and then eat a large meal at night. One of the most neglected meals is breakfast. Don't skip it, as the longest period of time without food is between the evening and the morning meals. Even during sleep the body uses energy to maintain essential bodily functions. At breakfast it is not necessary to eat a large cooked meal, but some nourishing food should be taken, for if you wait until lunchtime the body will go for over twelve hours without sustenance.

Pre-competition diet   During the last three or four days before a competition, it is important to top up the body stores by concentrating on a diet high in carbohydrates.

Competition diet   On the day of a match, eat food that is easily digested and take your last meal prior to playing two to three hours before the start. A small meal is ideal, so that it will not impair breathing. It should be high in carbohydrate but low in protein, as the latter is not easily digested. If exercise starts before this food is digested, the blood supply to the stomach will be shut off (the 'vascular shunt'), making you feel nauseous. Remember, fluid intake prior to the match is important.

Post-competition diet   Immediately after a hard match you may find that you cannot eat a heavy meal, especially if a large amount of fluid has been drunk. The first meal should be about one and a half to two hours after playing and should be rich in carbohydrates and protein.

Diet plays an important part in the life of squash players: most are on a 'see food diet' – they see food and eat it! Seriously, remember to eat at regular intervals, maintaining a balanced diet, not just 'junk' food.

Planning your training programme   First, it is vital carefully to plan your training around your work and home commitments to fit into the time you have available. In this way, you will gain the most benefit from your time. Second, always remember that it is squash for which you are training to get fit and don't get carried away with one type of training. Many club players only go out for long runs and wonder why these do not seem to help their game – they might help marathon runners, but not squash players.

Training must not only be a very personal thing, but it must also be relevant to the game of squash. We have already looked at the basic requirements: cardio-respiratory fitness, local muscle endurance, speed, some strength, agility and flexibility and the correct percentage of body fat. Remember that it is your weaknesses which let you down, so work hard on them, not just on your strengths which you probably enjoy training more.

If you are unable to devote very long to squash, the most useful approach is to spend time on court practising your racket skills, either on your own or with a partner. In conjunction with practice, concentrate on playing games as this will benefit you more than training away from the court. You should spend more time working on court than on off-court fitness training, unless you have an injury which prevents you playing. With most injuries, however, it is possible to do some form of training without causing further damage. Remember to heed medical advice as to the training you can safely do when injured.

Your training should be tailored to improve your fitness for squash, so that you can last a five-set match. Use the squash court for training, especially for ghosting sessions (see page 53). The majority of your training should be done during the close season, building up your stamina, improving your speed and strength. During the season, training should be lighter; if you continue to train too hard, you arrive on court drained, instead of sharp and ready to play.

Plan your year carefully and work out your training around it. Choose the tournaments in which you are going to play, being sensible not to overdo things by tiring yourself out rushing around the country without time to recover. Rest and recovery time are essential parts of a well-balanced fitness programme. Try to alternate hard days with easy days or even rest. There should be at least one complete day of rest a week to allow the body to recover. If you feel that you have to do something on your rest day, however, spend time doing passive stretching.

The key to a good training programme is progression, a gradual build-up. Don't expect miracles by suddenly doing a lot of hard work; the net result of this is often injury and a drained feeling. Remember to wind down in the fortnight before a major match or tournament.

It is a good idea to keep a training diary, recording what you did each day. In addition, make notes on how you felt before and after the training sessions. This can prove invaluable in planning for tournaments in the future, so you accurately know what worked for you and what did not.

If you have to miss days or weeks because of injury or illness, don't try to work harder to make up for lost time. Instead, start at a lower work rate than that to which you were accustomed before the lay-off and gradually build up again. Remember that a gradual progression will bring success.

All the different elements of your training programme should be balanced, especially if you do more than one session a day. Always do speed work first and an anaerobic session last, balancing a hard, intense anaerobic or explosive speed session with an easier aerobic session, a jog or swim. Don't do two hard sessions one after another as this is a recipe for disaster. Before and after every training session or game, warm up and then warm down.

Make passive stretching part of your daily routine, ideally morning and evening. The stretching part of your warming up not only helps to prevent injury but, if performed daily, improves your mobility on court too. If you have suffered any injury, it is vital to keep up the remedial exercises, even after the injury has healed. Remember that prevention is better than cure.

Time will dictate the amount of training you are able to do, but your weekly programme should ideally include:

1. Court practice of different types six days;
2. Aerobic training for endurance two or three days;
3. Anaerobic training two or three days;
4. Explosive speed training two or three days;
5. Muscle endurance training two days, possibly three;
6. Strength training two days, possibly three;
7. Flexibility work – stretching every day.

If you have a specific weakness, such as lack of speed, do more work in this area – perhaps four or five anaerobic and explosive speed sessions, with one to three aerobic sessions in between, in a week. If, however, you lack overall stamina, do more aerobic and circuit-training sessions, with less anaerobic and speed work. Remember to work harder at your weak areas than at your strengths, so improving your overall fitness.

Once the season draws to a close at the end of April, put your rackets down and have a rest in May, before starting your preparations for next season. The summer months of June, July and August are the months when you should be doing your background endurance work, the aerobic and anaerobic sessions, improving your cardio-respiratory capacity, local muscular endurance and strength. As you are moving into the last month of your three-month block of training, its quantity should decrease and its quality increase.

Jonah Barrington (Great Britain and Ireland) demonstrating an early preparation to attack the front of the court. (Photograph: Stephen Line)

Training programme graph.

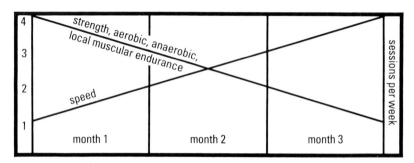

Speed work should figure more and strength and local muscle endurance training less.

If you are working towards a particular tournament during the season, you should time your build-up so that you can put in another phase of endurance work, 'fining down', in the time leading up to the tournament. This second heavy phase of training should be able to take you to a new level of fitness, building upon the foundations laid during the summer months. Don't try training flat out throughout the season and expect to play well at the same time. During the training phases you will feel tired and you will only reap the benefit of them once you 'fine down', hopefully peaking for the event you have been working so hard for.

Aerobic training for endurance

This type of training is often called 'steady state' work because it allows the working muscles to be in a 'steady state' – that is to get enough oxygen to convert the body's fuel into energy. It involves continuous activity over a period of time at between 75 and 90 per cent of your maximum effort, so that you are comfortably out of breath, but not working anaerobically. What you are aiming to do with 'steady state' training is to work the body hard enough to have a training effect.

Running

Start with short runs – five minutes if you are not a regular runner, or after a lay-off. Never attempt to run long distances immediately as this can cause blisters, severe stiffness or even injury, but over a period of weeks gradually build up to between twenty- and thirty-minute runs, trying to maintain a reasonably hard pace. Measure out a course of around about $3-3\frac{1}{2}$ miles and run this distance hard, timing yourself. If your trial time is, for example, twenty-five minutes, add 10 per cent to this time (two and a half minutes) to give you your training time (twenty-seven and a half minutes). You are then working at about 90 per cent of your maximum. After a month or less, if it is becoming easy, re-test yourself and set a new training time.

For running it is important to wear training shoes with well-cushioned soles. To absorb extra shock, use Sorbothane inner soles to replace the existing insole. Squash shoes are designed for the squash court, not for running; the soles are thin and totally unsuitable for this purpose.

Any repetitive training can cause injury, so as a preventive measure, vary the surfaces on which you run between road, grass cinder and synthetic running tracks. Try to avoid uneven surfaces, or always running the same way round your course: the camber of a road can cause problems, putting a strain on one side of the body.

If you are not a regular runner – that is, you have not been doing this sort of training for a year or more – don't run on consecutive days. Always allow at least one day between runs to give the body time to recover, so helping to prevent injury.

Cycling

Fifteen minutes of cycling is ideal to begin with, gradually building up to forty-five minutes. If you are using a static exercise bike, start with five minutes and build up to twenty minutes, using a moderate resistance. After the session, take your pulse, which should be raised to between 140 and 160 beats per minute.

To avoid any knee-cap pain, raise the saddle as high as possible, so that on the down sweep of the pedal the leg is almost straight. When using a moving bike, stand up in the pedals on inclines to prevent knee-cap pain. If your back aches after a session on either an exercise or moving bike, try raising the handlebars or altering the saddle height.

Skipping

Skipping is a very valuable method of training, not only for aerobic work but also for improving agility. Initially start with five minutes of skipping, using alternate feet, hopping from foot to foot on your toes. Try to keep up an even medium speed. Your target should be 1000 skips (500 each foot) every seven and a half minutes. Over a period of time, build up to about thirty minutes of skipping. Remember that if you have to skip on concrete, put down a piece of carpet and wear cushioned trainers, not squash shoes.

Swimming

Start with a ten-minute swim and build up to thirty minutes. When increasing your time in the water, ensure that you maintain a good pace. Your swimming effort should increase your pulse to about 120–130 beats per minute.

If you have any problems with your knees, swim crawl rather

than breast-stroke. Swimming can be a good substitute if an injury prevents normal training. Even if you are not a good swimmer, you can do exercises in the pool, like 'running' in chest-high water, gradually increasing the time and distance. After a heavy training session, swimming is a good way of loosening out stiff muscles. For those who suffer back problems, it is an excellent exercise.

Circuit training for endurance and speed

Circuit training is a combination of aerobic and anaerobic training. A well-balanced circuit, working each of your major muscle groups hard at speed, achieves not only an improvement in local muscle endurance but also in cardio-respiratory endurance (the efficiency of your heart/lung system).

Choose a number of exercises to be done in sequence to make up your circuit. Take care to balance the work throughout the body, alternating leg exercises with arm or trunk work. Start with ten or twelve separate exercises and do the circuit against the clock, going as fast as possible. As you are working against time, do not include heavy weights with the exercises. Try to ensure that you have plenty of space around you and that there are no pieces of equipment lying about which you could fall over.

Initially perform two circuits, going over the exercises twice. Gradually build up to a maximum of ten circuits, depending on how quickly you can perform the exercises chosen. Start with ten minutes' circuit training for your overall time and increase to a maximum of twenty-five to thirty minutes.

Circuit training should be designed to suit you like all your training. First, work out how many repetitions you do for each exercise in your circuit by performing each exercise for one minute as fast as possible, counting the number of repetitions. Do this for each exercise on your first circuit-training session to find your test rate. In between each exercise have one minute's rest so that you always work for a minute and rest for a minute. When starting your first session proper of circuit training, do all the exercises one after the other with no rest. To find your training rate, take the test rate for each exercise and halve it; for example, you might manage thirty sit-ups in a minute, so in training do fifteen.

Either every week or every fortnight repeat the minute test for each exercise to find your new test rate. This itself counts as a circuit session – you should not do circuit training more than two or three times a week.

After a while, if your circuit seems easy, simply add in more exercises. If it is only particular exercises that are too easy, begin to use *light* weights strapped to your wrists or ankles. Alternatively use sandbags or small dumb-bells. No matter how light the weights are, handle them carefully, remembering to bend the knees and keeping a straight back when lifting them.

It is important to keep a record of the exercises you do, the number of repetitions, the test rates and working rates, and any changes you make to them. Record the time taken for the circuits and your pulse rate immediately after the end of each session, and then your recovery rate at one-minute intervals for five minutes. Your recovery rate will be indicative of improvement in your fitness.

Explosive speed training

Speed is very important for a squash player: the quicker you reach the ball, the more time you have to steady yourself to hit it. Explosive speed training is designed to make you work as hard as possible without incurring the penalty of lactic acid in your muscles, as in anaerobic training. Remember to warm up thoroughly before you begin, however. This is particularly important prior to speed work: a torn or pulled hamstring is very painful and takes a long time to mend.

Start with ten-second bursts of intensive work, followed by fifty seconds' rest. The type of training should be gradually progressed (as with all forms of training), beginning with a small number of work and rest sessions – ten – and increasing the number session by session.

Court exercises, such as shuttle runs or shadow training, are good for the legs (see page 53). Away from the court, try 30-40 metre sprints on a running track or pitch, jogging back for the fifty seconds' recovery. Leg speed is more important to concentrate on, but don't neglect the arms. Do shadow strokes with your racket to improve your arm speed, or even while holding light weights (250–500 grams) in your hand. Alternatively, choose some of the arm exercises from the circuit list.

If you are able to do different types of training on the same day, the speed work should be done first. The principle of speed work is to train as fast as possible with maximum rest, so you need to be fresh when you start.

Anaerobic training

This trains your ability to work at high intensity, above the level at which your lungs and circulatory system can supply oxygen to the working muscles. Anaerobic training cannot be sustained for very long, so use stop-start bursts of activity/rest periods, enabling the waste products which your working muscles produce, such as lactic acid, to be removed. Anaerobic training improves the lactate removal system in your liver and kidneys.

A wide variety of exercises and activities are suitable for anaerobic training. Shuttle runs on court, sprints on a track or in the gym, fast skipping, sprint cycling, or any exercise or series of exercises may all be used, provided you can work hard enough at them.

If you are unaccustomed to anaerobic training, stiffness in the working muscles is almost inevitable if you have worked hard enough. It is therefore vital not to work these muscles again in the same way until they have recovered, as there is a risk of tearing them. Use passive stretching to ease them out little by little and do some other form of exercise, such as swimming, a relaxing way of loosening your muscles.

Interval training As the name suggests, this type of training is split between work and recovery. It is the most effective type of anaerobic training.

An easy formula is to work for thirty seconds, then rest for thirty seconds. Start with six intervals of intensive bursts of exercise (which can be shuttle runs, sprints, skipping or circuit exercises) alternated with rest periods. At each session add one extra work/rest interval until you have built up to twelve intervals. Once you are able to do this, work for thirty-five seconds with thirty-five seconds' rest, starting again with six intervals and building up by one per session to twelve. Following this, increase each interval to forty seconds and finally to forty-five seconds, as usual starting with six and building up to twelve. There is no real benefit in working for more than forty-five seconds as you will probably not be able to maintain the work intensively enough to achieve the anaerobic training effect.

If you are using shuttle runs in your interval training, be sure to count the number of stations per work session. Try to ensure that you maintain this standard for each of the work phases. Sometimes it is not always possible to time yourself, in which case try a distance run or a set number of skips. If using sprints for interval training, you can do these on a running track: sprint 200 metres, then jog/ recover back to the start. Begin with six sprints, building up to twelve, then increase the distance of the sprint and jogged recovery.

As a means of improving your anaerobic efficiency throughout the body's main muscle groups, choose a series of exercises from the circuit-training list (page 105). Ensure that these exercises cover all the main muscle groups and perform them against the clock, working at a high level of intensity with a timed rest period between each.

Remember that if you are going to do any other form of training during the day, always finish with anaerobic training.

You do not need to do heavy weight training because sheer strength beyond a reasonable amount is unnecessary for success in squash. You do, however, need to improve the local muscular endurance in the muscle groups you use, and this can be done through light weight training. Training with weights is *not*, however, suitable for juniors under the age of about sixteen to eighteen years, depending on body development.

Even if you are using a fixed weight system like a Multigym, you must still learn to handle the weights safely and do the exercises correctly. Start with extremely light loads so that you learn the techniques of each exercise. Even with a Multigym, never train without initial supervision from a trained instructor to ensure that you handle the weights properly. A resistance of 10 kilograms is all that is needed, if handled incorrectly, to slip a disc.

Balance your programme thoughout the whole body, working on legs, trunk and arms in turn, with the emphasis on your areas of weakness. Start with ten quick repetitions of each exercise and gradually (over a period of weeks or even months if you have not done any weight training before) work up to three sets of twenty repetitions. Aim to do each one as fast as possible, but ensure that you maintain good technique. Don't cheat for the sake of speed, because you will only cheat yourself.

With local muscular endurance training, resist the temptation to load the weight but use only whatever resistance you can comfortably handle on fast repetitions. Only when you can do each exercise at a particular weight easily should you increase the load, adding 2–5 kilograms, depending on the exercise. Some local muscle endurance exercises do not require weight training equipment because your own body weight can be used as the resistance – for example, in press-ups, chins to a bar, dips between parallel bars and sit-ups.

The Multigym system does provide stations for you to work through the body's main muscle groups. Remember when using the floor cord for the arm curls to bend your knees when pulling it from the floor and putting it down on completion of the exercises.

While using free weights, you must be supervised and 'spotted' (someone is at hand to take the weights from you when the set is finished). It is vital to handle weights with respect. When taking up the bar, always bend your knees and keep a straight back. Don't think, 'It is only a single weight; I don't need to worry.' Never do any exercise that involves bending forward or leaning over; the bent-over-rowing exercise is potentially damaging for your back. On completion of a set of a particular exercise, put the weight down correctly: this is as important as lifting correctly.

Muscle endurance work
Weight training and free exercises

The loading of weight to increase muscle endurance is only safe if you keep your spine as straight as possible. This means that you must not do specific weight-training repetitions simulating squash strokes – for example, practising strokes with increasingly heavy weights held in your hands or strapped to wrists. Specific muscle endurance will come from practising your skills. Any excessive over-loading of the working muscles in skill practices may cause loss of accuracy and ball control.

Muscle endurance work is designed to correct muscular imbalance, in addition to improving your playing strength. Therefore, if you have any particular problems, such as knee-cap pain, do straight-leg exercises in your programme, using light weights for some exercises. If you have back pain or stiffness, include plenty of back-extension exercises, progressing to using weights with them, and abdominal exercises for good musculature round the trunk. (See the circuit exercises on pages 107–8.)

Strength training

A certain amount of general body strength is, as already mentioned, required for squash. The areas to concentrate on are the wrist, upper arm and forearm, shoulders, chest, back, abdominals, quadriceps, hamstring and calf.

It bears repetition here that you must treat weights with respect. Stick to the rules – don't risk injury. Never use weights unless supervised by a trained instructor.

The principle of training with weights to increase strength is the opposite of local muscular endurance work, where you use light weights for a high number of repetitions. For strength training, use a high resistance with a lower number of repetitions. The way to work out your training weight for a particular exercise is to discover what you can lift, then take 80 per cent of it as your training weight. For example, if you can bench press for your pectoral muscles (chest) 50 kilograms, your training weight for that exercise is 40 kilograms.

For strength training, perform three sets of between ten and fifteen repetitions as quickly as possible on each exercise, working at 80 per cent of your maximum. In between each set, you can have as long a recovery as necessary to ensure that you are doing quality work. This type of training should be done during the summer months, beginning three months and finishing six weeks before the start of the season. Strength-training sessions should be done at least twice a week, but a maximum of three times a week, for six weeks. Balance the session, working arms, trunk and legs in rotation. Remember to make your strength training the last session in the day and don't try to play squash afterwards. It is important to finish this heavy phase of your training well before the season starts, to give your body time to recover.

This session can easily be done using a fixed-weight system, such as a Multigym:

General strength-training programme

1. Wrist rolling.

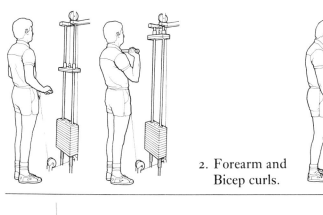

2. Forearm and Bicep curls.

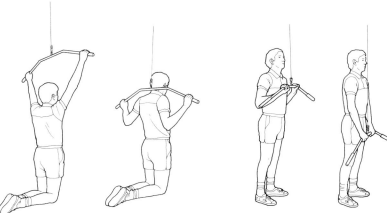

3. Shoulder – behind- and in-front-of-head press.

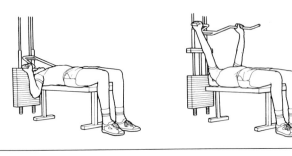

4. Bench press.

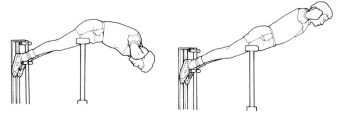

5. Back arches.

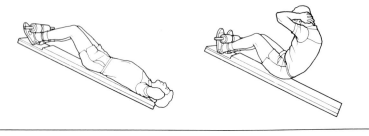

6. Sit-ups –
hands behind head
and bent knees.

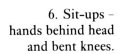

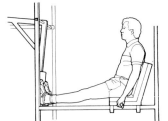

7. Leg press – quadriceps.

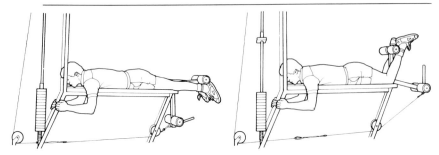

8. Leg curls –
hamstrings.

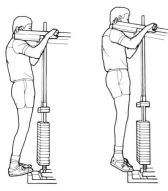

9. Calf raises – step on to a low bench (about 20 cm high) with a weight on your shoulders.

Perform three sets of between ten and fifteen repetitions, quickly but not at the expense of quality, working on 80 per cent of your maximum lifting capacity as resistance. Work your arms, trunk and legs in order.

1. Running on the spot.
2. Sprinting up and down stairs, or a slope.
3. Skipping.
4. Shuttle runs: sprint about 10 metres, touch the floor, sprint back.
5. Cycling on a static bicycle.
6. Leg lifts: sit on the floor, rapidly lift each leg straight up in the air in turn, keeping your knees locked straight.
7. Leg circling: sit on the floor, describe circles in the air first with one leg and then with the other, keeping your legs straight.
8. Semi-cycling: sit on the floor, bend one knee, keeping your heel on the ground and straighten the leg up, lifting your foot in the air; then lower, keeping the knee straight. Perform with each leg in turn.
9. Squats: standing, keep your back straight, bend your knees as far as is comfortable.

Circuit-training exercises
Legs

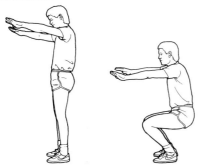

10. Toe-ups: standing, go up and down on your toes.
11. Alternate leg thrusts: crouching on the floor, take your weight on your hands and kick each leg out behind you in turn.

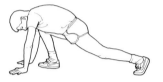

12. Squat thrusts: crouching on the floor, take your weight on your hands, and kick both legs together straight out behind you. Repeat, bending and straightening.

13. Burpees: as squat thrusts, but as you return to the crouch position, jump upwards straight into the air, returning to the squat position to re-start the movement.

14. Squat jumps: from squatting, touching the floor with your hands, spring upwards as high as you can, jumping down to touch the floor again in a continuous movement.

15. Step-ups: using a chair, bench or two stairs, preferably at least 50 cm high, step up with one leg, straightening the knee as the other leg is lifted up; step down with the same leading leg. Change the leading leg half-way through the repetitions.
16. Stand-ups A: using a low chair or bench, sit down and stand up from it, keeping your arms by your side.

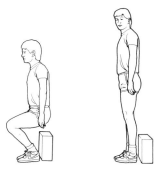

17. Stand-ups B: as for 'stand-ups A' but using one leg only, changing legs half-way through the repetitions.
18. Bench astride jumps: from standing with your legs on either side of a low bench, jump up to kick your heels together in the air above the bench and land with legs to either side of it.
19. Stand 30 cm from a wall with your back towards it, bend your knees to squat, and turn as you straighten up to touch the wall on each side behind you.

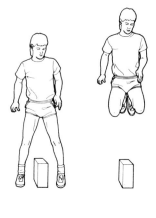

20. Hopping: hop forwards, then backwards, on each leg in turn.

1. Sit-ups: lying on the floor, with your hands resting on your thighs, lift your head and shoulders just enough to look at your toes, sliding your hands about 10 cm down towards your knees. (Do not sit right up.)

Abdominals

2. Lying on your back, with your arms by your side, bend your knees up and raise your head and shoulders until your elbows touch your knees. Straighten out more slowly.

3. Lying on your back, with your knees bent, feet on the floor and hands behind your head, lift your head and shoulders to touch each elbow in turn on the opposite knee.

4. Lying as in 3 (above), lift your head and shoulders to touch your knee with the opposite elbow, lower your head back, then repeat to the other side.

5. Lying on your back, with your arms above your head, holding a stick or pole and keeping your elbows straight, lift your arms forwards while bending up your knees; pass the stick under your feet and behind your knees, straightening your knees, then reverse the movement.

Back　1. Standing, with arms held straight out sideways, bend to each side in turn, with the upper arm behind the head.

2. Standing, with arms out sideways, turn to each side in turn.

3. Lying on your stomach, with your hands stretched out above your head, lift your arms, head and legs a little way from the floor, then lower. ·

4. Lying on your stomach, with your hands behind your head, lift your head and shoulders backwards and one leg backwards; lower, then lift head, shoulders and the other leg.

5. Lying on your back, with your knees bent and feet on the floor, lift your hips up to arch your back, then lower.

6. Lying on your back with knees bent and feet on the floor, swing both knees together towards each side in turn, keeping your feet and hips close to the floor.

1. Kneeling press-ups: kneeling on all fours, bend and straighten   *Arms*
   your elbows.

2. Press-ups.

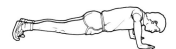

3. Backward press-ups: with your trunk and legs straight, supporting your upper body on straight arms resting on the floor behind you, bend and straighten your arms, keeping your body straight.

4. Curls: standing or sitting with light weights in your hands, bend your elbows, then straighten them out fully. Alternate your grip, doing one set with your palms facing downwards (overhand grip) and the next with your palms facing upwards (underhand grip).

Correct posture In your everyday life, try to maintain good posture at all times. Strains in muscles and joints, particularly in the back and neck, are often caused by bad posture; good posture can help to reduce the likelihood of this kind of injury now or later in life. Remember that prevention is far better than cure, so protect your body as much as possible. Be aware of adopting good habits when standing, sitting, lying and lifting.

There are two main factors that influence our everyday posture. First, gravity acts down against us when we are sitting or standing upright, and our muscles have to work to hold the body up. Second, virtually all people have a dominant side of the body, which in the case of squash players is more strongly developed, causing a muscular imbalance. Because you are using your dominant hand all the time, you accentuate this one-sidedness, creating more visible development in the size of your arm and down your back on the side in question. This is why it is so important, with local muscle endurance work, to develop both the left and right sides of the body equally.

Standing Stand evenly on both feet, trying to avoid balancing on one leg. Avoid slouching and keep your shoulders level. Try to keep your feet parallel or equally turned to avoid creating abnormal stresses to one of your hips.

Sitting Avoid sitting with your legs crossed, but try to keep your feet evenly placed on the floor. When sitting in a car seat or easy chair for any length of time, use a small cushion or rolled towel to support the curve of your lower back. Ensure that your chair and desk/table heights are matched when working, so that you are comfortably resting your elbows and forearms on the working surface, without having to lean down or reach upwards. From time to time, straighten up, stretching, to avoid stiffness.

You can create stresses in your joints by curling up or twisting in bed. When reading in bed, sit up supported; try to avoid lying on your side, propping up your head with your arm, or lying on your back bending your neck forward. Choose a bed that is comfortable for you, so it can adapt to your body contours.

Lying

Lift any weight by bending your knees and keeping a straight back. This is equally as important when using weights for training as when, say, picking up shopping. Avoid carrying a heavy weight in one hand without anything to balance it in the other.

Lifting

Fitness cannot be achieved overnight. A well-balanced, progressed training schedule is the only way to get fit, not only for squash but for any sport. Here are a few 'dos' and 'don'ts':

Safety and training

1. Never try to play or train through injury pain.
2. Never do exercises or activities that cause pain.
3. If you are ill, never exercise, especially with a temperature or muscle soreness before or after flu: you risk damaging your heart.
4. Keep a daily record of your pulse rate when you wake so that you know what your true resting pulse rate is. Then, if your rate on waking is raised by ten beats or more, and if you are not feeling well, do not train on that day and continue to rest until your resting pulse is back to normal and you are feeling well again.
5. When feeling run-down and over-fatigued before a session, and this feeling does not wear off during the activity, stop and rest until your energy returns; this may take a few days.
6. From time to time, you will have lay-offs for holiday, work, studies or illness. If this is the case, do not re-start your training schedule where you left off, but instead begin work again at a lower rate well within your limits and slowly build up over a period of a few weeks.
7. Eat meals regularly, taking a well-balanced diet (see page 90 for advice on nutrition). Do not fill yourself up with 'junk' food at the expense of eating proper meals. Try to have three meals a day rather than one large meal, overloading your stomach.

8. Do not train or play within two or three hours of a full meal.
9. Drink plenty of water when training and playing especially if prone to muscle cramp. Avoid fizzy drinks; plain water is much better. Experiment with electrolyte replacement drinks if you suffer badly from cramp.
10. Treat your body with respect: don't abuse it through over-exercising. Take care of it and reap the benefits of your training on the squash court.

A word of warning: juniors should do only a limited amount of training before the age of sixteen years.

The warm-up

How often do you see players warming up in your club's changing room before playing? Probably very rarely. Too many squash players arrive late for their match, with only just enough time to change into their kit and rush on to court. It is no wonder they become injured or don't perform to the level of their ability.

Warming up fulfils three basic functions: first, it helps to prevent injury; second, it improves the range of movement; and third, it prepares the body for the physical contest ahead. Bearing in mind the three reasons for warming up, it is hard to believe that players expect their body to function 100 per cent from 'cold'. A car doesn't: it needs choke until it warms up; the human body is the same, requiring to be slowly and carefully prepared for the battle ahead.

It is likely that many players don't warm up because they are embarrassed, as they think they are making fools of themselves. The less enlightened may find it amusing, but I can assure you that, if you persevere with warming up, you will have the last laugh. Remember the old saying 'prevention is better than cure'. Ten or fifteen minutes warming up before training or playing is preferable to weeks off with painful muscle pulls or tears. There are usually quiet places in clubs where you can go and hide away to warm up if you don't want to do it in full view of everyone in the changing room.

The warm-up should have three complementary stages to it: stretching exercises, mobilizing exercises and pulse warmers. This series should last approximately fifteen to twenty minutes – longer in cold weather. Consider the reason for each of the three stages in detail before concentrating on particular exercises.

Stretching exercises

The aim of stretching is to exercise the main muscles which are about to work. You are gradually trying to encourage the muscle fibres to lengthen, reducing tightness. See page 115 onwards for a list of exercises for specific areas of the body, and page 114 for a suggested exercise routine incorporating a selection of these.

Stretching should be performed statically, holding positions to feel a passive pull along the tissues being exercised. There is a right and wrong way to stretch: it is important, if you are to gain any benefit, that you don't 'bounce' up and down but that you maintain a relaxed sustained stretch position. The saying 'If it doesn't hurt, it isn't doing you any good' does not apply to stretching. Learn not to stretch to the point of pain, and certainly not through it. Progress is made by learning to relax gradually when stretching: over a period of days, weeks and months you will see the improvement.

What happens if you over-stretch a muscle by 'bouncing'? The body's 'stretch reflex' mechanism comes into play, in which an involuntary signal is sent to the muscle to contract, so preventing injury. You therefore end up by tightening the muscle, the very opposite result to that which you were trying to achieve; this reflex, over-stretching or bouncing can damage the fibrous support structure of the muscle, so always take care.

Aim to hold a stretch for a count of ten and repeat the exercise three times, but don't expect to be able to stretch further each time. Improvement is often slow and steady rather than rapid and spectacular. Be patient and persevere. Develop good habits when stretching. Although static, stretching does raise the muscle temperature by increasing the blood flow, but it is advisable to do a little jogging on the spot to warm up beforehand as muscles do stretch better when warm.

Mobilizing exercises

These should be rapid, free movements, to loosen the joints. Having stretched, you can safely start to mobilize the body with a series of exercises, again preparing it for the battle to come. These exercises can be done as many times as you like.

Pulse warmers

Finally, perform a series of fast-moving exercises to increase your cardio-respiratory functioning. When you start to exercise, you rapidly become short of breath, then after a short while you get the 'second wind' described earlier. The aim of the pulse warmers is to achieve this state prior to playing so that you avoid being at a disadvantage during the first rallies.

If you are planning to do 'steady state' training, pulse warmers are less important, but they must be done before a session of speed or interval training. Prior to a game of squash, pulse warmers must be performed as a game involves all three of the following: aerobic 'steady state', speed and intervals of anaerobic work.

Suggested routine   Here is an example of a warm-up routine which will help prevent injury, improve mobility and prepare your body for a match.

Stretching exercises   Hold each of the following for a count of ten and repeat at least three times, so that you can feel the stretch in the muscles.
1. Calves: lean forward to rest your hands against a wall with legs straight at hips and knees, and heels flat on the ground.
2. Quadriceps: balance on one leg, bend the other up behind you, keeping your hips well forward. Holding your ankle, pull your heel towards your seat.
3. Hamstrings: resting one leg forward on a support, reach forward towards your toes, bending from the hips, while keeping your head up. *Or* sitting, legs straight, bend forward from your hips. *Or* perform as adductor stretch 4 (below), but turn your toes upwards and lean over the outstretched leg, bending from the hips.
4. Adductors: stretch one leg out sideways and bend the other knee to the crouch position if possible, feeling the pull on the inside thigh of the straight leg.
5. Hip flexors: stretch one leg out backwards and bend forward on the other knee to the crouch position, keeping the back arched.
6. Shoulders: (a) bend one arm behind your head and hold the elbow with your other hand, gently pulling the bent elbow towards the other shoulder. (b) clasp your hands together behind your back, lift your arms straight back behind you and hold. (Keep your back as straight as possible.)
7. Anterior forearm: extend one arm straight in front of you, with the palm facing away from you and, holding the fingers of the outstretched arm with your other hand, gently pull them back towards you, keeping the elbow straight.

Mobilizing exercises   1. Arm circling and swinging: free large circular swings with both arms together or each in turn, alternating with swings forwards and backwards.
2. Knee bends: slow descent, fast push-ups, keeping back straight.
3. Trunk side-bending: with feet apart, bend from side to side, swinging your outside arm over your head as you bend.
4. Trunk turning: with arms held out sideways, swing from side to side, letting your outside elbow bend as you turn.
5. Hip circling: standing with feet apart, circle your hips, swinging your weight over each leg in turn.

Pulse warmers   These exercises should last between thirty seconds and one minute and each be performed quickly at least five times, each being followed by a fifteen- to thirty-second rest. The work/rest loads should vary, according to your own capacity. One exercise can be chosen and repeated, or a series of exercises: running on the spot, burpees, skipping, squat jumps or shuttle runs. The aim of pulse warmers is to achieve a continuous sequence of exercises and rest.

After completing the three phases of the warm-up, the stretching, mobility exercises and pulse warmers, spend a few minutes going over the swing. Without a racket in your hand, play an imaginary forehand, stepping into the ball, and the same on the backhand; then do the same with a racket in your hand. The aim of this is to groove your stroking action in preparation for going on to court for the knock-up. This helps to concentrate the body and mind, so both are working as one when you eventually hit the ball. Try it and see.

Grooving the swing

Just as important as the warm-up before training or playing is warming down, which helps to prevent muscular soreness the next day. It is the accumulation of waste-product fluids in the muscle tissues that cause stiffness in your limbs, and the warm-down – some gentle jogging and stretching – helps to continue the blood flow to the muscle tissue so that these waste-products are carried away. Discipline yourself therefore to warm down immediately after training, practising or a match, avoiding the temptation to head straight for the shower or bar. You will benefit from your warm-down the next day, especially if the match or training session has been hard.

Warming down

1. *Gastrocnemius, soleus and Achilles tendon stretch.* Lean forward to rest your hands against a wall. Place one leg behind the other, with feet parallel, and back heel flat on the ground. Bend the forward knee, until you feel a 'pull' on the calf of the hind leg. Hold for a count of ten, then slowly release. Repeat on the other leg.

Stretching exercises for specific areas of the body

Calf stretching

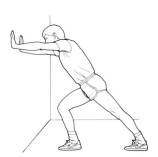

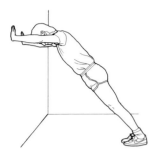

2. *Two-legged calf stretch*. Lean forwards against a wall or support. Move your legs backwards as far as you can while still keeping your heels flat on the ground. Hold for a count of ten.

3. *One or two-legged calf stretch*. Sit on the floor, with your legs straight out in front of you, or with one leg forward and the other tucked out of the way sideways. Reach down to hold one or both feet in your hands, keeping your knees straight, and pull your toes towards you with your hands. Hold for a count of ten.

4. *Soleus stretch*. Standing with your heels flat on the ground, bend both knees, letting your legs come as far down and over your ankles as you can, while keeping your heels flat on the ground. Hold.

5. *'Extra' calf stretch* (one or both legs). Place a block, 2.5–5 cm high, under your toes, or stand with your toes on a step, heels over the edge. Lean forward over your toes, letting your heels drop if you are on a step. Hold for a count of ten.

Quadriceps stretching

1. *Standing stretch*. Stand on one leg. Bend the other knee up, holding the ankle behind you with your hand. Pull the heel towards your buttock until you feel a 'pull' on the front of your thigh. Hold for a count of ten, then repeat on the other leg.

2. *Prone lying stretch*. Lying on your stomach, bend one or both knees, holding your ankle(s) in your hand(s). Press your heel(s) towards your seat. Hold.

3. *Kneeling stretch*. Kneeling, with knees and feet together, lean backwards as far as you can, pressing your hips forwards. Hold.

Hamstring stretching

1. *Two-leg sitting stretch*. Sit with your legs straight out in front of you. Reach down towards your feet or ankles with your hands. Lean forward from your hips, keeping your back as straight as possible and your head up. Hold.

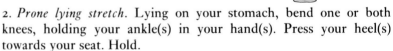

2. *One-leg sitting stretch* (hurdle position). Sit with one leg straight out forward, the other tucked out of the way sideways. Lean forward from the hips over the straight leg, with back straight and head up, and hold. Repeat over the other leg.

3. *Upward one-leg sitting stretch*. Sit with one leg tucked out of the way. Holding the foot of the other leg, straighten it upwards until you feel a 'pull' on the back of the thigh. Hold. Repeat with the other leg.

4. *One-leg standing stretch, with support*. Stand on one leg and place the other straight in front of you on a support (fence, chair). Hold your ankle or foot and bend forward from the hips, keeping your back straight. Hold, then repeat on the other leg.

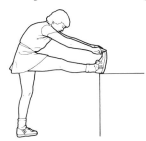

5. *One-leg stretch, crouching*. Bend one knee, steadying yourself with your hands if necessary. Stretch the other leg straight out sideways, with your foot pointed upwards. Lean over the straight leg from the hips, gently.

6. *Inner hamstring stretch, crouching*. Crouch down on one leg, as in 5 (above), with the other leg straight out sideways. Turn your foot so that the toes are at an angle of 45° with the ground. Lean over the straight leg. Hold. Repeat over the other leg. You will feel the 'pull' over the inner hamstring, on the inner side of the back of the thigh.

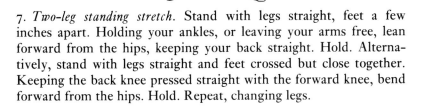

7. *Two-leg standing stretch*. Stand with legs straight, feet a few inches apart. Holding your ankles, or leaving your arms free, lean forward from the hips, keeping your back straight. Hold. Alternatively, stand with legs straight and feet crossed but close together. Keeping the back knee pressed straight with the forward knee, bend forward from the hips. Hold. Repeat, changing legs.

Adductor stretching

1. *Straight-leg sitting stretch.* Sit with legs straight and as far apart as possible. Lean forwards from the hips, keeping your back straight and head up. Hold.

2. *Bent-knee sitting stretch.* Sit with your knees bent and the soles of your feet together. Keeping your knees as close to the floor as possible, and holding your feet with your hands, lean gently forward from the hips. Hold.

3. *Crouching stretch.* Crouch down on one knee, placing the other leg straight out sideways. Keeping your foot parallel with the ground and your toes on the ground, lean gently towards the straight leg.

4. *Standing stretch.* Stand with your legs as far apart as possible. Shift your weight over one leg while leaning sideways over the other. Hold. Repeat over the other leg.

5. *Standing stretch with support.* Stand on one leg and, place the other straight out sideways on a support (chair, fence or block). Lean sideways over the raised leg. Hold. Repeat for the other leg.

Hip-flexor stretching

The hip flexors on the front of the thigh are stretched in combination with the quadriceps and abdominal muscles.

1. *Crouching stretch.* Bend one knee to the crouch position, placing the other leg straight back behind you. Arch your back, keeping your knee as straight as possible on the back leg. Hold. Repeat on the other leg.

1. Bend one arm behind your head. Hold the elbow with your other hand and gently pull the bent elbow towards the other shoulder.
2. Clasp your hands together behind your back. Lift your arms straight back behind you. Hold, keeping your back as straight as possible.
3. Clasp your hands together above your head, keeping your elbows straight. Take your hands back behind your head as far as they can go. Hold.
4. *Shoulder-girdle stretch.* Lie under a low bar, with your shoulders directly below the bar. Reach up to hold the bar, lifting your shoulders from the floor and keeping your arms straight. Hold the position, letting your shoulders relax downwards.
5. *Hanging stretch.* Hold a high bar, or the top of a door. Take your weight on your hands, letting your shoulders relax. Hold the position for as long as your hands are comfortable.

Shoulder stretching

1. *Anterior forearm stretch.* Hold one arm straight in front of you, with the palm facing away from you. Hold the fingers of the out-stretched arm with your other hand and gently pull the fingers back towards you, keeping your elbow straight. Hold. Repeat with the other arm.

Forearm stretching

2. *Posterior forearm stretch.* Bend the wrist and fingers of one hand. Use the other hand to bend the wrist even further, keeping the fingers bent. Hold. Repeat with the other wrist and hand.

Abdominal stretching

1. *Prone-lying stretch.* Lying on your stomach, place your hands directly under your shoulders on the floor. Straighten your elbows to arch your back as far as you comfortably can, arching your neck back. Hold.

2. *Prone-lying 'boat' stretch.* Lying on your stomach, bend your knees to a right angle and reach back to hold your ankles with your hands. Press your shoulders and feet upwards from the floor to arch your back. Hold.

3. *Lying stretch* ('crab'). Lying on your back, bend your knees, keeping your feet on the floor; bend your elbows beside your head, to place the palms of your hands on the floor under your shoulders. Push your trunk upwards, arching your back, so that your weight is balanced on your hands and feet. Hold.

4. *Kneeling stretch.* Kneeling with your knees close together, lean back as far as possible, keeping your hips well forward and head back. (Start by leaning on to your elbows; then aim gradually to be able to lean on your shoulders.)

Trunk stretching

1. *Forward stretch.* Sitting with your legs straight out in front of you, bend forward, trying to place your head between your knees. Hold.

2. *Twisting stretch.* Sit with one leg straight in front of you, and the other knee bent up, with the foot placed on the outside of the straight knee. Turn towards the bent knee, so that the opposite elbow rests on that knee to hold the twist position. Repeat to the other side.

3. *Side-bend stretch.* Standing, reach down to one side, letting the opposite arm bend over the top of your head. (Keep facing forward.) Hold. Repeat to the other side.

Practice: the way
to perfect your game

5

It is very important, if you want your game to improve, to practise. A spectator watching Gary Player, the great South African golfer, play a remarkable recovery shot from a bunker, remarked, 'How lucky can you be!' In reply Gary Player is reported to have said, 'The more I practise, the luckier I become.' So the next time your opponent calls you a lucky . . . . ., you know what to say!

When I was learning to play the game, my coach was always urging me to practise and not to waste my time on court. He told me of the story of how, when he arrived at a club in London to play, he saw Jonah Barrington on court practising on' his own, working on the cross-court volley nick. He kept feeding the ball up, then hitting it into the nick, mumbling under his breath if he made a mistake. When my coach came off court, Jonah was still working on the same shot over an hour later. Knowing the utter dedication of the greatest squash player to come from this country, I can believe this story.

I am not suggesting, however, that you spend over an hour on court just practising one shot, but it is vital that for any shot to be played successfully in a match, you have to hit hundreds in practice. When the ball is in a certain position in a match and you go for a particular shot, you can do so with confidence knowing you've hit it many times in practice.

The first time I was invited to coach one of the Squash Rackets Association national under-14 and under-12 squads, Alan Colburn – then South African National Coach - came along as a guest. As the boys sat around on the floor, listening to him talk, three points on the subject of practice struck home with me as well as with those eager young squash players: practise your weaknesses, pay attention to detail, and perfect practice makes perfect.

First, practise your weaknesses. I have already stressed that, because it is not your strengths that are going to let you down in match play but your weaknesses, you should concentrate harder on practising the latter. Discipline yourself to spend your time trying to eradicate your weaknesses and bring this area of your game up to near the level of your strengths. Of course, don't neglect your strengths – do spend some time working at them as well – but not at the expense of weaknesses, as it is these that your opponent is going to attack. Make his life as difficult as possible by developing a sound all-round game.

Second, pay attention to detail. It is not going to help your game if you practise the poor technique that is contributing to the errors you make in match play. Try at all times to concentrate when you have time in practice to play the shot correctly. Don't be sloppy: this is often reflected in your match play.

Third, perfect practice makes perfect. If you are doing a practice that requires a certain court movement, make sure you do it properly and don't cheat. Remember that, if you do, you are only cheating yourself. Do the practice properly to get maximum benefit from it. Watch the top players working on court and you will soon realize why they are at the top. Jahangir Khan is very disciplined on the practice court and his results in tournaments aren't bad! Watch Jonah Barrington too – he still drives himself when working on his own or with 'Bomber' Harris, and hates to make a mistake. I am not suggesting that you have to concentrate totally on squash to the exclusion of everything else in life, but just a little of the dedication of these players can help you to achieve your goal.

Quality must be your watch word. I have always been suspicious of players I coach who say they spent over an hour working on their own the other day, then proceed to put the ball consistently in the tin. Thirty or forty minutes of quality is worth far more than an hour or more of just knocking the ball around. Set yourself targets, therefore, for each shot you are going to practise. Put actual targets down on the floor too, so that you are not just aimlessly hitting, but are trying to strike a particular area on the floor. At a junior national squad weekend, one of the players put a small piece of white tape on the ball, so that he had something on which to focus his attention when practising. He felt that this helped to improve the quality of his practising: why not try it yourself?

Make practising competitive, so that it is disciplined, not sloppy. Invent a scoring system, perhaps scoring a point for every good shot and losing one for every poor one or each mistake. Set yourself a number to achieve before moving on to practise the next shot. Jonah Barrington, for example, when working on his drop shot, feeds the ball from the 'T' in a variety of ways, then moves in to play a winning drop, as though it were the final of the British Open, calling out the score after each shot and urging himself on to greater efforts. This typifies practising with a purpose to me: it's far more than just going through the motions. He is totally engrossed in what he is doing, unaware of what is going on outside his match – Barrington v. Barrington.

If you are feeding for a partner, give him every chance by feeding accurately. Again, be competitive: see how many attempts he needs to hit a set number of nicks or lengths into a target, or how often you are unable to return his shot.

To assist you in your practice, guidance is given on the following pages for practising drives, volleys, boasts, service and return, lobs, drops and kills (solo, in pairs and in threes).

Drives
Solo

With each of these four practices, aim to beat your best score.

1. Continuous rally, aiming to bounce the ball in the service box.
2. Continuous rally, aiming to bounce the ball behind the service box.
3. Continuous rally, aiming to keep the ball going after it bounces and hits the back wall.
4. Standing on the 'T', hit the ball across your body on the forehand so that it strikes front wall, and the side wall in the front left corner. Then play a backhand, hitting across your body and aiming to hit the front wall and the side wall in the front right corner to bring the ball back to the 'T'.

Pairs

1. Player A feeds the ball short from behind the back of the service box for Player B to drive the ball to a length. Aim for ten shots into a target, then reverse roles.
2. Rallying, aim to bounce the ball behind the short line and between the edge of the service box and the side wall. The more accurate you become, the narrower you should make the target area. Put a small target on the floor within the area, scoring a point every time either of you hits it and taking a point off every time either fails to return the ball into the half-length narrow strip.
3. Drive/boast. Player A plays a boast for Player B to drive the ball to a length. Player A then boasts from the other side of the court. The aim is for Player B to hit twenty drives into a target on either side of the court before changing roles.
4. Player A feeds the ball short for Player B to drive the ball to a length. Player A then feeds a length ball for Player B to hit a drive to length, followed by a short feed. Then the roles are reversed. This is a good exercise for teaching players to hit good tight width and length, otherwise the feeder can cut the ball off too easily, putting pressure on his practice partner. This can be made competitive, with the feeder against the player driving the ball to length.

5. As in 4 (above), but both players drive the ball to length, moving up and down the court. Player A feeds short, Player B drives to length. Player A hits length again, B then hits short for A to hit length and the practice continues.

6. Player A feeds short, long, then a boast for Player B to drive the ball to a length, enabling Player B to practise hitting length drives from all four corners of the court.

7. As in 6 (above), but Player A can random the feed for Player B to hit length drives.

Threes 1. Player A and Player B stand behind the service box with a ball each, feeding shorts for Player C on the 'T' to move from side to side, driving the ball to a length first on the forehand, then on the backhand. Pressure can be increased on Player C by cutting down the time between feeds.

2. As in 1 (above): one feed short, one feed deep for Player C to move forward then across and back to drive the ball to a length.

Cross-court drives It is difficult to practise cross-court drives effectively on your own.

Solo 1. Stand on the 'T', feed the ball short and then drive it cross-court, aiming to strike the side wall low around the back of the service box.

Pairs 1. Player A feeds forehand boasts from the back of the court for Player B to move from the 'T' to play backhand drives cross-court. Repeat on the other side of the court.

2. Player A feeds straight drops for Player B to drive the ball cross-court, so both forehand and backhand shots can be practised.

3. Both players rally straight down one wall until able to cross-court, aiming for good width, so the ball cannot be cut off; then the rally continues down the opposite side wall till one player is able to cross-court.

4. Player A boasts for Player B to drive the ball cross-court. Player A then hits the ball straight for Player B to boast for a cross-court drive to be played by Player A.

Service Practise lob, semi-lob, drive and hard-hit serves. Remember to con-
Solo centrate on hitting the target areas for these serves.

Pairs These practices involve return of service. Both service and return service are very neglected areas of the game, so it is vital that both shots are practised regularly.

1. Player A serves and Player B returns the ball to length either straight or cross-court. Player A then plays another shot.
2. As in 1 (above), with the rally continued in a restricted area of the court.

1. Standing about a yard from the front wall, volley continuously.
2. Standing on the short line, volley continuously.
3. Standing behind the back of the service box, hit continuous shoulder high or above volleys.
4. Standing on the 'T', forehand volley across your body so that the ball hits the front wall and side wall, then backhand volley to hit the front wall and side wall, keeping the rally going as for the drives.

Volley
Solo

1. Player A stands on the 'T' and Player B feeds the ball from behind the back of the service box for Player A to volley the ball to a length.
2. Player A feeds one straight then one cross-court shot from the back of the court for Player B to volley straight.
3. As in 2 (above), but Player A feeds only cross-court shots.
4. Player A can feed either straight or cross-court shots for Player B to volley straight.
5. Player A feeds from one back corner, either straight or cross-court, for Player B to volley the ball back to the feeder, to practise straight and cross-court volleys.
6. Rallying down the side wall, both players trying to dominate the short line by volleying the ball.
7. Each player stands on one side of the court on the short line, volleying the ball via the front wall back and forth to each other.
8. As in 7 (above), with both players standing around the back of the service box, practising high volleys.

Pairs

1. Player A stands on the 'T', and Players B and C stand behind the back of the service box with a ball each, feeding alternately for Player A to volley straight to a length.
2. As in 1 (above), but with one low feed and one high feed for Player A to volley to a length.
3. Player A boasts, Player B drives cross-court and Player C tries to volley the ball straight to a length.

Threes

1. Hand feed, standing behind the back of the service box, to play a boast, pick the ball up and re-feed.
2. To practise the boast out of the back corner, hand feed the ball so that it hits the side wall and then the back wall.

Boast
Solo

3. Rally the ball up and down the side wall, then boast.

Pairs 1. Player A plays a cross-court drive from the front left-hand corner for Player B to play a boast out of the opposite back corner.
2. Player A plays straight drives from the front of the court for Player B to play alternate forehand and backhand boasts.
3. Player A can play either straight or cross-court drives for Player B to play boasts.
4. Player A plays a cross-court drive for Player B to play a boast. Player A plays a drop, Player B plays a short angle, then Player B drives deep for A to boast.
5. Player A can play either straight or cross-court drives and Player B boasts; off the boast a short or long feed is played by Player A for Player B to boast again.
6. Player A drives for Player B to volley boast.

Threes 1. Player A plays cross-court drives for Players B and C to take it in turn to boast the ball.
2. Players A and B stand at the front of the court, driving straight for Player C to boast the ball.
3. Players A and B drive alternately straight or cross-court for Player C to boast the ball.

Lob 1. Feed the ball short to play a straight lob.
Solo 2. Feed as in 1 (above) to play a cross-court lob.
3. From the short line, boast to feed for a straight or cross-court lob.

Pairs 1. Player A, standing at the back of the service box, feeds short for Player B to move from the 'T' to play a straight lob.
2. Player A plays boasts from the back of the court for Player B to play straight lobs, alternating forehand and backhand.
3. Player A plays a boast for Player B to play a cross-court lob, repeating from the other side of the court.
4. Player A feeds short, straight or with a boast for Player B to play straight or cross-court lobs.
5. As in 4 (above), but Player A can feed any shot short for Player B to lob straight or cross-court.
6. Player A boasts, Player B cross-court lobs, Player A hits a straight volley, for B to boast, then A lobs.

Threes 1. Players A and B with a ball each feed alternately short for Player C to lob straight.

2. As in 1 (above), but Player C lobs cross-court.

3. Player C can lob straight or cross-court. Players A and B feed either short, straight or boast using one ball.

4. Player A boasts, Player B lobs cross-court for Player C to volley straight. They then repeat, changing the shot played.

Drop

Solo

1. Feed the ball short from the 'T' to play a straight drop.

2. Feed the ball across your body to hit the front wall and the side wall, and turn to play a straight drop.

3. Feed as in 2 (above) to play a cross-court drop.

4. Play high boasts from the 'T' to play straight drops.

5. Feed the ball, varying it to drop in front of the short line to play straight or cross-court drops.

6. Feed the ball to bounce in the service box to play more heavily cut straight drops.

7. As in 6 (above), but for cross-court drops.

8. Play over-hit drives to play straight drops from the back of the court.

Pairs

1. Player A feeds from the front of the court a ball bouncing midway between the front wall and the short line for Player B to play straight drops. Player B must remember to move from the 'T' and recover after each shot.

2. As in 1 (above), but varying the length so that a shorter feed is succeeded by one bouncing in the service box.

3. As in 2 (above), with random length of feed, working Player B up and down the length of the court.

4. Player A feeds from the front left-hand corner for Player B to hit cross-court drops, varying the feeds so that some are short and some deeper, but keeping the ball in front of the short line.

5. Player A boasts and Player B straight drops, moving from the 'T'. B simply feeds the ball back to A to boast again.

6. Player A boasts, Player B straight drops, Player A drives straight, Player B boasts.

7. Player A boasts, Player B plays a weak drop, Player A drops straight, Player B hits cross-court for A to boast.

8. As in 7 (above), but with Player A varying the feed for straight drops off a ball bouncing between the front wall and the service box.

Threes

1. Players A and B, with a ball each, feed alternately for Player C to move from side to side, playing straight drops at the front of the court.

2. As in 1 (above), but with Player C returning to the 'T' after each shot.

3. Using one ball, Players A and B feed cross-court drives for Player C to play straight drops from half- to three-quarter court.

4. Player A boasts, Player B drops straight, Player C hits a straight drive. The positions are rotated.

5. As in 4 (above), except that Player B drops cross-court.

Kills
Solo

1. Easy set-up from the 'T', bouncing the ball above the height of the tin to play a straight kill into the nick.

2. As in 1 (above), but hitting cross-court.

3. Feed the ball deeper to bounce in the service box, again bouncing above the tin to kill the ball into the nick.

Pairs

1. Player A sets up an easy feed from the back of the court for Player B to kill the ball straight into the nick.

2. As in 1 (above) for a cross-court kill into the nick.

3. Player A feeds a weak high boast for Player B to kill straight or cross-court into the nick.

Threes

1. Players A and B, with a ball each, feed high-bouncing balls alternately for Player C who moves from side to side from the 'T' to kill the ball into the nick.

Short volleys
Solo

1. Standing on the 'T', feed the ball up to volley it hard and low, aiming it into the nick in the front corner.

2. As in 1 (above), but aiming to volley the ball cross-court into the nick in the front corner.

3. As 1 and 2 (above), but aiming to take the pace off the ball, playing a drop volley and working on cutting the ball with an open racket face to take the pace off it.

Pairs

1. Player A plays a straight lob from the front of the court for Player B to move from the 'T' to play a straight drop volley.

2. As in 1 (above), but Player A drives the ball for Player B to drop volley.

3. As 1 and 2 (above), but Player A varies the height and pace of the ball for Player B to drop volley.

4. Player A feeds from behind for Player B to play straight volley kills, aiming into the nick.

5. Player A feeds short cross-court lobs from the front left corner for Player B to play volley kills cross-court into the nick.

6. As in 5, but Player B to drop volley cross-court into the nick.

7. Player A feeds alternately cross-court lobs for Player B to drop volley straight.

8. Player A lobs straight or cross-court for Player B to drop volley straight.

9. As in 8 (above), but Player B can drop volley straight or cross-court.

1. Players A and B, with a ball each, alternately feed easy balls from behind the service box for Player C to volley kill straight, aiming for the nick.

2. As in 1 (above), but Player C plays straight drop volleys.

3. All three players stand down one side wall. Player A feeds a weak lob from the back of the court for Player B on the 'T' to cut off with a drop volley. Player C drives to the back for Player B to cut off with a length volley. Player A lobs.

Threes

Include condition games in your practice to work on a particular element of your game. These can be very useful when working with a player who is better than you. Below are some examples.

Condition games

1. Both players must hit the ball to bounce behind the short line.

2. One player plays normally, the other can only hit length, i.e. the ball to bounce behind the short line.

3. As in 1 (above), but restrict the area at the back of the court to the width of the service box or less.

4. One player plays normally, the other can only hit straight.

Length games

1. Working on one side of the court only and using the service box width, play length only, i.e. everything must bounce behind the short line.

2. One player can play long or short for the other to hit length only.

3. Both players, using the whole length of the court, play both long and short.

Alley games

1. Defending the back wall. Neither player must let the ball bounce and then hit the back wall, or he will lose the rally. This encourages both players to volley. If the ball hits the back wall on the full, continue the rally.

2. Both players hunt the ball to volley, scoring an extra point for each volley.

3. Both players win an extra point if they win a rally with a volley.

Volley games

Target game. Aim to bounce the ball in the shaded areas.

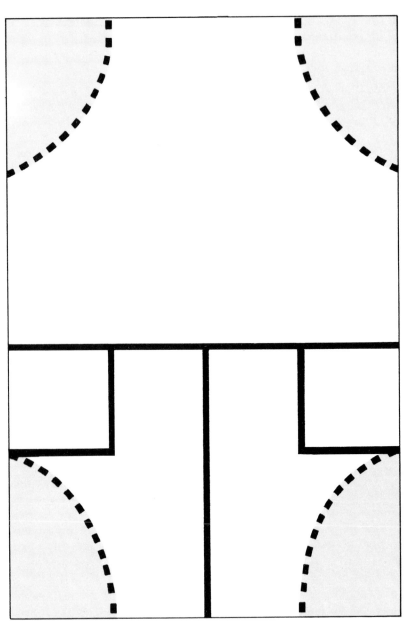

Cross-court games   1. One player plays normally, the other plays everything cross-court, either long or short. A boast does not count as a cross-court shot.

Boasts   1. One player plays normally, the other can only play boasts or angles.

1. One player plays normally, the other must play every shot to bounce in front of the short line, straight or cross-court.
2. A harder variation which Jonah Barrington and 'Bomber' Harris play is that Jonah can only play straight and short.
3. Drop-shot game in front of the short line, both players playing straight or cross-court drops.
4. One player plays normally, the other plays the first rally length only and the next short only. Continue alternating long and short rallies. This certainly keeps you thinking!

1. Both players lose the rally if either plays a shot which lands outside the alleys on either side of the court, using the service-box width for the alley or a narrower one, depending on the ability of players.
2. Every shot must bounce in one of four large targets set in each corner of the court (see illustration).

6

The mental approach – it's all in the mind

What have Jonah Barrington, Geoff Hunt and Jahangir Khan in common, apart from the first two being former world champions and Jahangir being the current world champion? The answer is mental toughness, a trait possessed by all world champions in any sport. That's what makes them stand out, head and shoulders above the rest. There is a saying in sport: 'When the going gets tough, the tough get going,' and this is certainly true. Those who were privileged to watch Jonah Barrington in his prime will remember the matches when it seemed he wouldn't score a point, but he hung on, fighting his way back into the match to win.

Geoff Hunt showed the same fighting qualities in the final of the British Open in 1981 against the current world champion Jahangir Khan. Hunt won the first two games, dominating his younger opponent with his relentless length and volleying. However, the pace began to tell and Hunt started to fade, letting the younger player back into the match. At two games to one up, Hunt was again in trouble in the fourth, but somehow he managed to raise the pace with one more supreme effort. I doubt Jahangir could believe that his older opponent could raise his game. Hunt won the fourth game to take the British Open Championship for a record-breaking eighth time, to the delight of a packed Churchill Theatre in Bromley.

There was no doubt that Hunt was in trouble in the fourth and Jahangir was dominating the rallies. Hunt must have felt that, if he was hurting, probably Jahangir was as well, so if he could raise the pace he would break his younger opponent mentally – which in fact he did. In your matches, when in trouble physically, always try to make one more effort to raise your game, because psychologically this can have a shattering effect on your opponent. Once you are again picking up points, it is surprising how you find energy from somewhere. Never say die, fight to the very end – many a match has been won from 2–0 and 8–0 down.

Match preparation is very important. As stressed earlier, always give yourself plenty of time to reach a tournament venue. If you don't, it should not surprise you if you find yourself one game down and struggling in the second before you know what is happening.

Assuming that you have prepared yourself physically as well as

Geoff Hunt (Australia) British Open Champion for a record eight times. (Photograph: Stephen Line)

possible for a match, how should you prepare mentally? It is important to be a little nervous: this is the adrenalin letting the body know that 'battle' is about to commence. Without this reaction, you would probably not be ready mentally and physically to play. Players who are not 'hyped up', not mentally alert, often perform well below their best, and seem unable to get going at all. The problem occurs when your anxiety level goes over the top, as this affects performance: often you hear sports commentators say that this player or that never reproduces his form on the big occasion. Many top sportsmen and sportswomen use sports psychologists to help them prepare mentally. They know that nerves are a good thing, but there is a thin line between success and failure. Anxiety – being too nervous – can drain a player, making even the best mover in the world appear wooden and rooted to the spot, unable to move and hit the ball freely.

Gillian Gilks, the former world champion badminton player, used to get so nervous before a big match that she was often physically sick and, consequently, didn't perform at her best. Her coach used two methods to calm her down before matches, and both worked well. Meditation was tried first – he used to get her to sit quietly, concentrating on each part of the body in turn, to relax her totally. The net result was that she was totally relaxed when she came to play. This worked for a season, until she realized what was happening, and could no longer concentrate on the different parts of her body, because the match took over in her mind. Next her coach tried a vigorous warm-up followed by a hard knock-up on court, and then she went straight on to court to play the match. She prepared herself for the match not only physically by stretching the muscles and mobilizing the joints, but also mentally by getting her mind in tune with her body, by hitting shuttles prior to going on to the match court.

Unfortunately, in tournaments or inter-club matches, it is rarely possible to have the luxury of a practice court. However, there should be nothing to stop you from being able to do a vigorous warm-up. By becoming totally involved in the warm-up, you can prepare yourself mentally as well as physically.

Whichever way you choose to prepare for your match, make sure you give yourself time to do so. On the other hand, try to avoid spending forty-five minutes to an hour on the balcony marking, then going straight on to court to play, cold and not alert mentally.

All the top players approach their matches differently. Some outwardly appear very calm and relaxed; others talk incessantly; while others still show different obvious signs of tension. Find a pre-match routine that is right for you, whether it is the quiet meditation method or the vigorous warm-up, or a combination of both. Prepare yourself so that you are 'hyped up' for your match, but not 'over the top' and too anxious.

In the match itself, consider how vital a part concentration and self-discipline can play. You're prepared mentally and physically, so there should be no excuses for playing badly. Remember that it is impossible to play badly if you are sound on the basics. You may not win, but if you discipline yourself not to make mistakes and always perform the simple things well, you won't play badly.

Right from the start of the match, develop what I call 'tunnel vision': don't allow any outside influences to affect your play. Total concentration on the job in hand is needed – ignore the crowd and the antics of your opponent, and accept referees' decisions, no matter how bad you feel they are. In fact, develop a 'poker face', so that your opponent never knows what you are thinking about.

Bjorn Borg was the acknowledged past master at disguising his thoughts and feelings. Mentally he controlled himself superbly, right from the start of his matches. Good habits off court breed good habits on the court and Borg was a prime example of this. He didn't let anything affect his game. But even Borg did not always used to be so calm: he taught himself to control his emotions and reaped the rewards.

There are vital periods in games when squash matches are won or lost. A good start is essential, aim to dominate your opponent, make it physically tough for him, get inside his head and make him worry. From this good start, don't let your opponent back into the match, but keep your concentration, pushing home your advantage.

Many matches are often even up to 6 all or 6-5, and then one player pulls away to win. This stage in a game is critical, for a lapse in concentration can make the difference between winning and losing. The better player at this stage will step up his work rate to win. Players often have a word, a mantra, they repeat silently to themselves over and over again to help them concentrate their mind on the game; they use this whenever they feel their mind wandering. Evonne Cawley, the great Australian tennis player, a winner of Wimbledon, often described herself as 'going walkabout' in matches. Use this concentration technique if you feel yourself 'going walkabout' in your own games.

From the moment the marker calls 'love all' in the first game until the last point is won, complete concentration is essential. Go along and watch any league match at your club and I guarantee that one or both players will throw away two or three points at some stage or other, because they let something distract them. It may be a referee's decision, or even a bad shot which dwells in their mind. This lapse of concentration could be the difference between winning and losing the game, or even the match. Once a rally has ended, or a referee has made a decision, nothing you can do will change the outcome, so forget it and concentrate on the next rally – don't let what has happened affect you for the next two or three rallies.

Learn to concentrate on each rally regardless of the game or match score. Take each rally one at a time, rather than letting the state of the match impose itself on your mind, so affecting your performance. Borg, one year at Wimbledon, was two sets to love down against Vijay Amritaj of India, with his opponent in a position to win the match. A lesser player would have folded, but Borg battled on, winning in the fifth set. In the post-match interview, he was asked what he was thinking about, staring defeat in the face. His reply was that he shut out the state of the match and played each point one at a time till he won a game and continued in the same vein, eventually winning in the fifth set. Bjorn Borg had the ability to stay calm in a crisis and come through.

Before the start of a match, clear your thoughts of your last match, no matter whether you played well or badly. In this way you will go on to court without any prior expectation of playing as you did in your last game. Don't prejudge your performance on the basis of what has gone before. If, during your previous match you played well, going on to court trying to reproduce this form means you are not concentrating on the match in hand. On the other hand, if you played badly the last time, this too can prey on your mind, so again your concentration wanders: one bad performance compounds another. Go on to court concentrating on the present, not trying to recreate, or thinking about, the past.

Once you are well into the match, how should you approach the hardest rally, the moment when you are at match point? When serving for the match, try not to think about the fact that it is match point, but concentrate on each shot, one at a time. Don't let the state of the match take over in your mind. Try to avoid thinking, 'Just one more point to win', as this can upset your concentration. Winning the last point in a match can be harder than the first, because an opponent on the brink of defeat will often fight harder, so don't make life difficult for yourself. Play the rally out taking each shot in turn, concentrating on playing positive squash.

Many sportsmen and sportswomen often produce performances which are far and above their normal level but, try as they may, they cannot repeat this higher level at will, it comes and goes. In tennis Borg was described as being 'in the zone', in other words he was hitting the ball as though on automatic pilot. Phrases like 'playing unconscious', 'in the zone' and 'spacey' are often used to describe such a feeling of being on automatic pilot, playing on another plain. Golfers often experience 'seeing a shot before they play it'; they visualize the flight path of the ball and where it is to land, then select the club and reproduce what they have 'seen'.

In the United States and also in the communist bloc countries, research into the physiology of the brain has shown that there are two different types of consciousness. The first is to do with what we term 'rational' thinking; the second is concerned with imaginative processes of thought and intuition. In her book *Playing on their Nerves* (Stanley Paul, 1979), Angela Patmore describes the two faculties of the brain as 'B' and 'A'. Mike Brearley said in an article in *The Times* that if only he could let go and trust his body, his batting would improve. In other words, you can't think and hit at the same time. That's why learning a new skill is often very difficult, because you are concentrating so much on what you should be doing that you forget the all-important thing, which is to hit the ball – i.e., stay in 'A' not in 'B'.

Fast bowlers in cricket rely heavily on keeping the rhythm going in their run-up and delivery stride, so staying in 'A'. If the bowler starts to think about what he is doing, his rhythm is lost. The same philosophy applies to all sport; the harder you try to reproduce a performance by really concentrating rather than letting your body take over, the more likely it is that the end result will suffer.

Tim Gallwey's 'inner game' philosophy (*The Inner Game*, Jonathan Cape, 1975) is based on the belief that a player has two selves related to the 'B' and 'A' parts of the brain, which he calls 'Self 1' and 'Self 2'. Self 1 is the thinker, which gives instructions and tells you off when you make a mistake. Self 2 is the automatic pilot, the unconscious thought process of the brain. Gallwey believes that we should try to free Self 2 from Self 1's interference, so allowing the body to take over and play. When we refer to someone as 'playing unconscious', meaning that he is in a state of total concentration and does not have to think what to do, he has let Self 2 take over. The problem arises when Self 1 insists on interfering and giving orders, such as when a player makes a mistake and calls out – this is Self 1 blaming his body for the error. In your games, try letting Self 2 rule; don't clutter your mind by thinking too much about how you are going to hit the ball. Help this to happen by putting bad shots behind you and not dwelling on them. Don't let Self 1 take over and cause more unforced errors.

Gallwey also believed that it is possible to programme Self 2 like a computer to carry out instructions through a series of images. The trick is to show Self 2 a number of mental images of what is required. If Self 1 lets go, Self 2 will reproduce these pictures. This process of letting go *may* need as much practice as would a particular technique, i.e. a player no doubt would practise fifty forehands, but would he practise letting go in fifty matches? Gallwey used the idea of focusing attention on a particular object, the ball, so shutting out Self 1. In squash, try imagining the dot on the ball – this has the same effect as a mantra repeated over and over again to focus one's attention. Self 2 has taken over, so letting you play in an unconscious state, and the mind can concentrate on the job in hand without continual interference from Self 1.

The aim of all this is to produce a state of relaxed concentration, so that you, the player, are able to perform to the best of your ability. Occasionally, if you are lucky, you may have the experience of 'playing unconscious', 'in the zone', or 'spacey'. Everyone at some time has had the experience of playing a superb shot, then wondering how on earth they did it and finding they were unable to repeat it immediately. This is when the automatic pilot has taken over, or Self 2, or 'A' – or whatever you want to call it. Remember: you can't hit and think at the same time.

Look at the ideas in the chapter to see if they help to improve your game. Mental as well as physical preparation for a match should be an important part of your build-up. Mental preparation is a very personal thing; try the meditation technique or the vigorous warm-up to relax you before going on to court. Once involved in a match, strive to achieve the state of relaxed concentration, letting your body take over so you are flowing.

It really is all in your mind!

The rules of the international singles game of squash rackets

Approved by the ISRF at its AGM in October 1984, to become effective 1st September 1985.

1. The game, how played. The game of squash rackets is played between two players, each using a standard racket, with a standard ball and in a court constructed to ISRF standard dimensions.

2. The score. A match shall consist of the best of 3 or 5 games at the option of the organisers of the competition. Each game is to 9 points, in that the player who scores 9 points wins the game except that, on the score being called 8 all for the first time, the receiver shall choose, before the next service is delivered, to continue that game either to 9 points (known as 'No set') or to 10 points (known as 'Set two'), in which latter case the player who scores 2 more points wins the game. The receiver shall in either case clearly indicate his choice to the marker, referee and his opponent.

The marker shall call either 'No set' or 'Set two' as applicable before play continues.

3. Points, how scored. Points can be scored only by the server. When the server wins a stroke, he scores a point; when the receiver wins a stroke, he becomes the server.

4. The service. 4.1 The right to serve first is decided by the spin of a racket. Thereafter the server continues to serve until he loses a stroke, whereupon his opponent becomes the server, and this procedure continues throughout the match. At the commencement of the second and each subsequent game, the winner of the previous game serves first.

4.2 At the beginning of each game and each hand, the server has the choice of either box and thereafter shall serve from alternate boxes while remaining the server. However, if he serves a fault which the receiver does not attempt to return, or a rally ends in a let, he shall serve again from the same box. If the server does serve from the wrong box, play shall continue and the service shall count as if served from the correct box, except that the receiver may, if he does not attempt to return the service, require that it be served from the correct box.

Note to markers. If it appears that the server intends to serve from the wrong box, or either player appears undecided as to which is the correct box, the marker shall indicate to the server the correct box.

4.3 For a service to be good, there must be no foot-fault and the ball, before being struck, shall be dropped or thrown in the air and shall not hit the walls, floor, ceiling or any objects suspended from the walls or ceiling; it must be served direct onto the front wall between the cutline and the out line, so that on its return, unless volleyed, it reaches the floor within the back quarter of the court opposite to the server's box. Should a player, having dropped or thrown the ball in the air, make no attempt to strike it, it shall be dropped or thrown again for that service. A player with the use of only one arm may utilize his racket to propel the ball into the air before striking it.

4.4 A service is good when it is not a fault (Rule 4.5) or does not result in the server serving his hand out (Rule 4.6). If the server serves one fault, which the receiver does not attempt to return, he shall serve again. The receiver may attempt to return a fault on the first service and, if he does so, that service becomes good, is no longer a fault and the ball continues in play. A second service fault cannot be played by the receiver.

Note to referees. The referee shall decide what is an attempt to play the ball.

4.5 A service is a fault:

4.5.1 if at the time of striking the ball the server fails to have part of one foot in contact with the floor within the service box and no part of that foot touching the service box line (called a foot-fault). Part of the foot may project over this line provided that it does not touch the line.

4.5.2 if the ball is served on to or below the cut line but above the board.

4.5.3 if the first bounce of the ball, unless volleyed, is on the floor on or outside the short or half-court lines delineating the back quarter of the court opposite to the server's box.

Any combination of types of faults in the one service counts as only one fault.

4.6 The server serves his hand out and loses the stroke:

4.6.1 if he serves two consecutive faults.

4.6.2 if the ball touches the walls, floor, ceiling or any object(s) suspended from the walls or ceiling before being served.

4.6.3 if the server makes an attempt but fails to strike the ball.

4.6.4 if, in the opinion of the referee, the ball is not struck correctly.

4.6.5 if the ball is served onto or below the board, or out, or

'Let, please,' asks Jahangir Khan in the 1984 World Masters in Warrington. (Photograph: Stephen Line)

141

against any part of the court before the front wall.

4.6.6 if the ball, before it has bounced more than once on the floor or before it has been struck at by the receiver, touches the server or anything he wears or carries, whether the service was otherwise good or a fault.

4.7 The server shall not serve until the marker has completed calling the score.

Note to officials. The marker must not delay play by the calling of the score. However, if the server serves, or attempts to serve, prior to the calling of the score, the referee shall stop play and require the server to wait until the calling of the score has been completed.

5. The play. After a good service has been delivered the players return the ball alternately until one fails to make a good return, the ball otherwise ceases to be in play in accordance with the rules, or on a call by the marker or referee.

6. Good return. A return is good if the ball, before it has bounced more than once upon the floor, is returned correctly by the striker onto the front wall above the board, without first touching the floor or any part of the striker's body or clothing, or the opponent's racket, body or clothing, provided the ball is not hit out.

Note to referees. It shall not be considered a good return if the ball touches the board before or after it hits the front wall, or if the racket is not in the player's hand at the time the ball is struck, or if the ball is carried on the racket.

7. Let. A let is an undecided stroke, and the service or rally in respect of which a let is allowed shall not count and the server shall serve again from the same box. A let shall not cancel a previous fault.

8. Strokes, how won. A player wins a stroke:

8.1 under Rule 4.6, when the player is the receiver.

8.2 if the opponent fails to make a good return of the ball, unless a let is allowed or a stroke is awarded to the opponent.

8.3 if the ball touches his opponent or anything he wears or carries when the opponent is the non-striker, except as is otherwise provided by Rules 6, 9, 10 and 13.1.1.

8.4 if a stroke is awarded to him by the referee as provided for in the rules.

9. Hitting an opponent with the ball. If the ball, before reaching the front wall, hits the striker's opponent or his racket, or anything he wears or carries, the ball shall cease to be in play and:

9.1 if the ball would have made a good return and would have struck the front wall without first touching any other wall, the striker shall win the stroke except if the ball, after rebounding from the front wall, strikes a side wall and the striker follows the ball round and so turns, or without so turning, allows the ball to pass around his body, in either case taking the ball on the hand opposite to that of the side wall from which the ball rebounded, then a let shall be allowed.

Note to referees.

A. This includes the case where the striker plays the ball behind his back or between his legs.

B. If the striker, having turned, or allowed the ball to pass around his body, chooses not to continue the rally due to the possibility of striking his opponent and, in the opinion of the referee, is able to make a good return, then a let shall be allowed.

9.2 if the ball either had struck or would have struck any other wall and would have made a good return, a let shall be allowed unless, in the opinion of the referee, a winning stroke has been intercepted, in which case the striker shall win the stroke.

Note to referees. Where the striker has turned or allowed the ball to pass around his body, a let shall be allowed.

9.3 if the ball would not have made a good return, the striker shall lose the stroke.

Note to officials. When a player has been struck by the ball as described in Rule 9, the marker shall call 'Down'. The referee shall assess the trajectory of the ball and make all further decisions.

10. Further attempts to hit the ball. If the striker strikes at and misses the ball, he may make further attempts to strike it. If, after being missed, the ball touches his opponent or his racket, or anything he wears or carries, then if, in the referee's opinion:

10.1 the striker could otherwise have made a good return, a let shall be allowed, or

10.2 the striker could not have made a good return, he loses the stroke.

If any such further attempt is successful, resulting in a good return being prevented from reaching the front wall by hitting the striker's opponent or anything he wears or carries, a let shall be allowed in all circumstances. If any such further attempt would not have made a good return, then the striker shall lose the stroke.

11. Appeals. Appeals to the referee under Rule 11 should be made with the words 'Appeal, please'.

In all cases under Rule 12 where a let or a stroke is desired, an appeal should be made to the referee with the words 'Let, please'. Play shall then cease until the referee has given his decision. If an appeal under Rule 11 is disallowed, the marker's decision shall stand. If the referee is uncertain he shall allow a let except where provided for in note to referees on Rule 11.2.2. Appeals upheld are dealt with in each specific situation below.

Note to referees. Players making a pointing gesture during a rally should be advised that such action is not a recognized form of appeal.

11.1 Appeals on service.

11.1.1 An appeal may be made against any decision of the marker except for a call of 'Fault' or 'Foot-fault' to the first service.

11.1.2 If the marker fails to call 'Fault' or 'Foot-fault' to the first service, the receiver may appeal provided he makes no attempt to play the ball. If the appeal is upheld the service shall be a fault.

11.1.3 If the marker calls 'Fault' or 'Foot-fault' to the second service, the server may appeal. If the appeal is upheld, a let shall be allowed, with 'one fault' standing.

11.1.4 If the marker fails to call 'Fault' or 'Foot-fault' to the second service the receiver may appeal, either immediately or at the end of the rally if he has played the ball. If the appeal is upheld, the receiver shall win the stroke.

11.1.5 If the marker calls 'Out', 'Not up' or 'Down' to either first or second service the server may appeal. If the appeal is upheld, a let shall be allowed.

11.1.6 If the marker fails to call 'Out', 'Not up' or 'Down' to either first or second service the receiver may appeal, either immediately or at the end of the rally if he has played the ball. If the appeal is upheld, the receiver shall win the stroke.

Note to referees. If the marker has not called 'One fault' prior to the delivery of a second service and that service is a fault the receiver, if not awarded the stroke, may appeal that the service was a second service, either immediately or at the end of the rally if he has played the ball. If the appeal is upheld, the receiver shall win the stroke.

11.2 Appeals on play, other than service.

11.2.1 An appeal may be made against any decision of the marker.

11.2.2 If the marker has called the ball 'Out', 'Not up' or 'Down' following a player's return, the player may appeal. If the appeal is upheld a let shall be allowed, except that if in the opinion of the referee:

the marker's call has interrupted that player's winning return, he shall award the stroke to the player.

the marker's call has interrupted or prevented a winning return by the opponent, he shall award the stroke to the opponent.

Note to referees. In the latter case the referee shall also award a stroke to the opponent if he is unsure whether the marker's call was correct.

11.2.3 When the marker has failed to call the ball 'Out', 'Not up' or 'Down' following a player's return, the opponent may appeal either immediately or at the end of the rally if he has played the ball. If the appeal is upheld, the referee shall award the stroke to the opponent.

Note to referees.

A. No appeal under Rule 11 may be made after the delivery of a service for anything that occurred before that service.

B. Where there is more than one appeal in a rally, the referee shall consider each appeal in the order in which the situations occurred.

C. If a return is called 'Not up' by the marker and subsequently goes 'Down' or 'Out', the referee, on appeal, if he reverses the marker's call, or is unsure, shall then rule on the subsequent occurrence.

12. Interference.

12.1 After playing a ball, a player must make every effort to get out of his opponent's way. That is:

12.1.1 a player must make every effort to give his opponent a fair view of the ball.

12.1.2 a player must make every effort not to obstruct the opponent in the latter's direct movement to the ball. At the same time the opponent must make every effort to get to, and where possible play, the ball.

12.1.3 a player must make every effort to allow his opponent freedom to play the ball.

Note to referees. The freedom to play the ball must include a reasonable backswing, strike at the ball and a reasonable follow-through.

12.1.4 a player must make every effort to allow his opponent, as far as the latter's position permits, freedom to return the ball directly to the front wall, or to either side wall to within approximately one metre of the front wall.

If a player fails to fulfil one of the requirements of Rule 12.1 (1 to 4) above, whether or not he has made every effort to do so, then interference will have occurred.

12.2 If any such form of interference has occurred and, in the opinion of the referee, the player has not made every effort to avoid causing it, the referee shall on appeal, or on stopping play without waiting for an appeal, award the stroke to his opponent, provided the opponent was in a position to make a good return.

Note to referees. In the case of Rule 12.1 the appeal must be immediate.

12.3 However, if interference has occurred but in the opinion of the referee the player has made every effort to avoid causing it, and the opponent could have made a good return, the referee shall on appeal, or on stopping play without waiting for an appeal, allow a let, except that, if his opponent is prevented from making a winning return by such interference from the players, the referee shall award the stroke to the opponent.

Note to referees.

A. A player who plays on despite interference forfeits the right of appeal concerning that interference.

B. Where a player's opponent creates his own interference, the referee shall rule that interference has not occurred unless the player has contributed to it.

12.4 When, in the opinion of the referee, a player refrains from playing the ball which, if played, would clearly have won the rally under the terms of Rule 9.1 or 9.2, he shall be awarded the stroke.

12.5 If either player makes unnecessary physical contact with his opponent, the referee may stop play, if it has not already stopped, and award the stroke accordingly.

Note to referees.

A. The practice of impeding an opponent in his efforts to play the ball by crowding or obscuring his view is highly detrimental to the game. Unnecessary physical contact is also detrimental as well as being dangerous. Referees should have no hesitation in enforcing Rules 12.2 and 12.5.

B. The words 'not to obstruct' in Rule 12.1.2 must be interpreted to include the case of an opponent having to wait for an excessive follow-through of the player's racket.

C. A player's excessive backswing may create interference when his opponent has made every effort to avoid such interference. In this case if the player appeals for a let he shall not be awarded the stroke.

D. When, in the opinion of the referee, a player's swing is excessive and is considered to be dangerous, the referee shall apply Rule 17.

13. Let, when allowed.

13.1 A let may be allowed:

 13.1.1 if, owing to the position of the striker, the opponent is unable to avoid being touched by the ball before the return is made.

 Note to referees. This rule shall be construed to include the cases where the striker's position is in front of his opponent and makes it difficult for the latter to see the ball, or where the striker shapes as if to play the ball but changes his mind at the last moment, preferring to take the ball off the back wall, and the ball in either case hits his opponent, who is between the striker and the back wall. This is not, however, to be taken as conflicting in any way with the duties of the referee under Rule 12.

13.1.2 if the ball in play touches any article lying on the floor.

Note to referees. Referees must ensure that no articles are placed on the floor by the players.

13.1.3 if the striker refrains from hitting the ball owing to a reasonable fear of injuring his opponent.

Note to referees. This rule shall be construed to include the case of the striker wishing to play the ball onto the back wall.

13.1.4 as provided for in Rule 12.

13.1.5 if, in the opinion of the referee, either player is distracted by an occurrence on or off the court.

Note to referees. This shall include the case of an obvious late call on the first service by the marker.

13.1.6 if, in the opinion of the referee, court conditions have affected the result of the rally.

13.2 A let shall be allowed:

13.2.1 if hand-out is not ready, and does not attempt to return the service.

13.2.2 if the ball breaks during play.

13.2.3 if the referee is asked to decide an appeal and is unable to do so.

13.2.4 if an otherwise good return has been made, but the ball goes out of court on its first bounce.

13.2.5 as provided for in Rules 9, 10, 11, 16.1, 17, and 19.5.

In order for a let to be allowed in any of the Rules 13.1 (2 to 6) and 13.2.5 above, the striker must have been able to make a good return.

13.3 No let shall be allowed when the player has made an attempt to play the ball except where the rules definitely provide for a let, namely Rules 9, 10, 11, 13, 16.1, 17 and 19.5.

13.4 Unless an appeal is made by one of the players, no let shall be allowed except where the rules definitely provide for a let, namely Rules 9, 10, 12, 13, 16.1, 17 and 19.5.

14. The ball.

14.1 If a ball breaks during play, it shall be replaced promptly by another ball.

Note to referees. The referee shall decide whether or not a ball is broken.

14.2 At any time, when the ball is not in actual play, another ball may be substituted by mutual consent of the players, or on appeal by either player, at the discretion of the referee.

Note to referees. Either player or the referee may examine the ball at any time it is not in actual play, to check its condition.

14.3 If a ball has broken but this has not been established during play, a let for the rally in which the ball broke shall not be allowed once either the receiver has attempted to return the next service or the server has served his hand-out with that service.

14.4 Where a player wishes to appeal about a broken ball, the appeal must be made before the next service is returned by the receiver or, if it is the final rally of the game, immediately after the rally.

14.5 If a player stops play during a rally to appeal that the ball is broken only to find subsequently that the ball is not broken, then that player shall lose the stroke.

15. Warm up

15.1 Immediately preceding the start of play, the referee shall allow on the court of play a period of 5 minutes to the two players together for the purpose of warming up the ball to be used for the match.

With $2\frac{1}{2}$ minutes of the warm-up remaining, the referee shall advise the players that they have used half their warm-up time with the call 'Half-time' and ensure that they change sides unless they mutually agree otherwise. The referee shall also advise when the warm-up period is complete with the call of 'Time'.

In the event of a player electing to warm up separately on the court of play, the referee shall allow the first player a period $3\frac{1}{2}$ minutes and his opponent $2\frac{1}{2}$ minutes. In the case of a separate warm-up, the choice of warming up first or second shall be decided by the spin of a racket.

15.2 Where a ball has been substituted under Rule 14 or when the match is being resumed after considerable delay, the referee shall allow the ball to be warmed up to playing condition. Play shall resume on the direction of the referee, or upon mutual consent of the players, whichever is the earlier.

Note to referees. The referee must ensure that both players warm up the ball fairly (Rules 15.1 and 15.2). An unfair warm-up shall be dealt with under the provisions of Rule 17.

15.3 Between games the ball shall remain on the floor of the court in view and shall not be hit by either player except by mutual consent of the players.

16. Continuity of play.

After the first service is delivered, play shall be continuous so far as is practical, provided that:

16.1 At any time play may be suspended, owing to bad light or other circumstances beyond the control of the players, for such period as the referee shall decide. The score shall stand.

If another suitable court is available when the court originally in use remains unsuitable, the match may be transferred to it if both players agree, or as directed by the referee.

In the event of play being suspended for the day, the score shall stand unless both players disagree in which case the match shall start again.

16.2 An interval of 1 minute shall be permitted between games and of two minutes between the fourth and fifth games of a five-game match. A player may leave the court during such intervals but shall be ready to resume play by the end of the stated time. When 15 seconds of the interval permitted between games are left, the referee shall call 'Fifteen seconds' to warn the players to be ready to resume play. At the end of the interval between games the referee shall call 'Time'.

It is the responsibility of the players to be within earshot of the court to hear the calls of 'Fifteen seconds' and 'Time'.

Note to referees.

A. Should one player fail to be ready to resume play when 'Time' is called, the referee shall apply the provisions of Rule 17.

B. Should neither player be ready to resume play when 'Time' is called, the referee shall apply the provisions of Rule 17 for both players.

16.3 If a player satisfies the referee that a change of equipment, clothing or footwear is necessary. The referee may allow the player to effect the change as quickly as possible with a maximum allowance of 2 minutes. If the player fails to return within the allotted time, the referee shall apply the provisions to Rule 17.

16.4 In the event of an injury to a player, the referee shall decide if it was:

16.4.1 self-inflicted.

16.4.2 contributed to accidentally by his opponent, or

16.4.3 caused by the opponent's deliberate or dangerous play or action.

Note to referees.

A. In 16.4.2 and 16.4.3 above, the referee must determine that the injury is genuine.

B. The referee must not interpret the words 'contributed to accidentally by his opponent' to include the situation where the injury to the player is as a result of that player occupying an unnecessarily close position to his opponent.

In Rule 16.4.1 above the referee shall require the player to continue play; or concede the game, accept the minute interval and then continue play; or concede the match.

In Rule 16.4.2 above the referee shall allow reasonable time for the injured player to recover having regard to the time schedule of the competition.

In Rule 16.4.3 above the referee shall award the match to the injured player.

16.5 The referee shall award a stroke, game or match to the opponent of a player, who, in his opinion, persists, after due warning, in delaying the play unreasonable. Such delay may be caused by:

16.5.1 unduly slow preparation to serve or receive service,

16.5.2 prolonged discussion with the referee, or

16.5.3 delay in returning to the court having left under terms of Rules 16.2 and 16.3.

17. Conduct on court.

If the referee considers that the behaviour of a player on court could be intimidating or offensive to an opponent, official or spectator, or could in any other way bring the game into disrepute the player shall be penalised.

Where a player commits any of the offences listed in the Rules 12.5, 15.2 and 15.3, 16.2 and 16.3 or the ISRF Code of Conduct (Appendix 6.) The following penalty provisions may be applied:

warning by the referee,

stroke awarded to opponent,

game awarded to opponent, or

match awarded to opponent.

Notes to referees.

A. If the referee stops play to give a warning, a let shall be allowed.

B. If the referee awards a game, that game shall be the one in progress or the next game if one is not in progress. The offending player shall retain any points already scored in the game awarded.

18. Control of a match.

A match is normally controlled by a referee, assisted by a marker. One person may be appointed to carry out the functions of both referee and marker. When a decision has been made by the referee, he shall announce it to the players and the marker shall repeat it with the subsequent score.

Note to officials. Having only one official to carry out roles of both marker and referee is undesirable.

Up to 30 minutes before the commencement of a match either player may request a referee and/or marker other than appointed, and this request may be considered and a substitute appointed. Players are not permitted to request any such change(s) after the commencement of a match, unless both agree to do so. In either case the decision as to whether or not an official is to be replaced must remain in the hands of the tournament referee or adjudicator where applicable.

19. Duties of a marker.

19.1 The marker calls the play followed by the score, with the server's score first. He shall call 'Fault', 'Foot-fault', 'Out', 'Not up' or 'Down' as appropriate, and shall repeat the referee's decisions.

19.2 If, in the course of play, the marker calls 'Not up', 'Out', or 'Down' or in the case of a second service, 'Fault' or 'Foot-fault', the rally shall cease.

Note to markers. If the marker is unsighted or uncertain he shall make no call.

19.3 Any service or return shall be considered good unless otherwise called.

19.4 After the server has served a fault, which has not been accepted for play, the marker shall repeat the score and add the words 'One fault', before the server serves again. This call shall be repeated when the subsequent rally ends one or more times in a let, until the stroke is finally decided.

19.5 If play ceases, and the marker is unsighted or uncertain, he shall advise the players and shall call on the referee to make the relevant decision; if the referee is unable to do so, a let shall be allowed.

Note to markers. Markers must use recognized marker's calls including when the rally has ceased. (Appendix 1.1).

20. Duties of referee.

20.1 The referee shall allow lets and award strokes; make decisions where called for by the rules, including when a player is struck by the ball and for injuries; and shall decide all appeals, including those against the marker's calls. The decision of the referee shall be final.

20.2 The referee shall not intervene in the marker's calling except:

20.2.1 upon appeal by one of the players.

20.2.2 as provided for in Rules 12 and 17, or

20.2.3 when it is evident that the score has been called incorrectly, in which case he shall have the marker call the correct score.

Note to officials. It is recommended that both marker and referee record the score.

20.2.4 If he is certain that the marker has made an error in stopping play or allowing play to continue, he shall immediately rule accordingly.

20.3 The referee is responsible for ensuring that all times laid down in the rules are strictly adhered to.

20.4 The referee is responsible for ensuring that court conditions are appropriate for play.

20.5 In exceptional cases the referee may award a stroke, a game or the match to the opponent of a player whose conduct is in his opinion detrimental to the match in progress and the game of squash in general. The referee may also order:

> *20.5.1* a match to be awarded to a player whose opponent fails to be present on court ready to play, within 10 minutes of the advertised time of play.

> *20.5.2* play to be stopped in order to warn that the conduct of one or both of the players is leading to an infringement of the rules.

Note to referees. A referee should avail himself of this rule as early as possible when either player is showing a tendency to break the provisions of Rules 12, 16.5 or Rule 17.

Rule changes approved by the International Squash Rackets Federation to come into effect from the 1st May 1989:

One serve rule with the cut line in play.
90-second interval between all games.
Elimination of provision for separate warm-up.
Elimination of provision for players to change referees.
Deletion of reference to the 1 metre of side wall.
Deletion of reference to ball having to hit side wall for it to be turning.

Appendix 1.1

Definitions

Adjudicator Responsible for the conduct of players and officials throughout the tournament.

Appeal A player's request to the referee to consider an on or off court situation. 'Appeal' is used throughout the Rules in two contexts:

> (1) where the player requests the referee to consider varying a marker's decision and,

> (2) where the player requests the referee to allow a let.

Correct form of appeal by player is 'Let, please' or 'Appeal, please.'

Board The board is the lower horizontal line marking on the front wall, with the 'tin' beneath it for the full width of the court.

Box (service) A square delineated area in each quarter court, bounded by part of the short line, part of the side wall and by two other lines and from within which the server serves.

Competition A championship, tournament, league or other competitive match.

Correctly The ball being hit by the racket (held in the hand) not more than once nor with prolonged contact on the racket.

Cut line A line upon the front wall, the top edge of which is 1.83 metres (6 feet) above the floor and extending the full width of the court.

Down The expression used to indicate that an otherwise good return has struck the board or has failed to reach the front wall. ('Down' is used as a marker's call).

Game Part of a match, commencing with a service by server and concluding when one player has scored or beeen awarded 9 or 10 points (in accordance with the Rules).

Game ball The state of the score when server requires one point to win the game in progress. ('Game ball' is also used as a marker's call.)

Half-court line A line set upon the floor parallel to the side walls, dividing the back of the court into two equal parts, meeting the 'short line' at its midpoint, forming the 'T'.

Half-time The midpoint of the warm-up (also used as a referee's call).

Hand (As referred to in Rule 9.1) A player's racket hand position in regard to its approximate location on one side or the other of his body at the moment of ball contact with the racket, a hand on the right side of his body (if facing the front wall) being right and on the left side, left.

Hand-in The period from the time a player becomes server until he becomes receiver.

Hand-out Condition when change of server occurs. ('Hand-out' is also used as a marker's call to indicate that a change of hand has occurred.)

Match The complete contest between two players commencing with the warm-up and concluding when both players have left the court at the end of the final rally. (Covers broken ball rule.)

Match ball The state of the score when hand-in requires one point to win the match. ('Match ball' is also used as a marker's call.)

Not up The expression used to indicate that a ball has not been struck in accordance with the Rules. 'Not up' covers all returns which are not good and are neither 'down' nor 'out' – with the exception of 'faults' and 'foot-faults'. ('Not up' is also used as a marker's call.)

Out The expression used to indicate that a ball has struck the out line or a wall above such line or the roof, or has passed over any part of the roof (e.g. cross bars). ('Out' is also used as a marker's call.)

Out line A continuous line comprising the front wall line, both side wall lines and the back wall line and marking the top boundaries of the court.

Note: When a court is constructed without provision of such a line, i.e. the walls comprise only the area used for play, or without the provision of part of such a line (e.g. a glass back wall), and the ball in play strikes part of the horizontal top surface of such a wall and deflects back into court, such a ball is out. Because of the difficulty in ascertaining just where the ball strikes the wall, the decision as to whether such a ball is out should be made by observing the deflection back into court – an abnormal deflection indicating that the ball is out. This decision should be made in the normal manner by the marker, subject to appeal to the referee.

Point A unit of the scoring system. One point is added to a player's score when he is server and wins a stroke.

Quarter (court) One half of the back part of the court which has been divided into two equal parts by the half court line.

Rally Series of returns of the ball, comprising one or more such returns. A rally commences with a service and concludes when the ball ceases to be in play.

Reasonable backswing The initial action used by a player in moving his racket away from his body as preparation prior to racket movement forward towards the ball for contact. A backswing is reasonable if it is not excessive. An excessive backswing is one in which the player's racket arm is extended towards a straight arm position and/or the racket is extended with the shaft approximately horizontal. The referee's decision on what constitutes a reasonable as distinct from excessive backswing is final.

Reasonable follow-through The action used by a player in continuing the movement of his racket after it has contacted the ball. A follow-through is reasonable if it is not excessive. An excessive follow-through is one in which the player's racket arm is extended towards a straight arm position with the racket also extended with the shaft horizontal – particularly when the extended position is maintained for other than a momentary period of time. An excessive swing is also one in which the arm extended towards a straight position takes a wider arc than the continued line of flight of the ball, even though the racket shaft is in the correct vertical position. The referee's decision on what constitutes a reasonable versus excessive follow-through is final.

Referee (tournament) Tournament referee is given overall responsibility for all marking and refereeing matters throughout the tournament including the appointment of officials to matches.

Service The method by which the ball is put into play by the server to commence a rally.

Short line A line set out upon the floor parallel to and 5.49 metres (18 feet) from the front wall and extending the full width of the court.

Standard The description given to balls, rackets and courts that meet existing ISRF specifications.

Stop Expression used by the referee to stop play.

Striker The player whose turn it is to hit the ball after it has rebounded from the front wall, or who is in the process of hitting the ball, or who – up to the point of his return reaching the front wall – has just hit the ball.

Dimensions of a singles court *Appendix II*

Length 9.75m (32ft)
Breadth 6.40m (21ft)
Height to upper edge of cut line on front wall 1.83m (6ft)
Height to lower edge of front-wall line 4.57m (15ft)
Height to lower edge of back-wall line 2.13m (7ft)
Distance to further edge of short line from front wall 5.49m (18ft)
Height to upper edge of board from ground 0.48m (19in)
Thickness of board (flat or rounded at top) 12.5–25mm ($\frac{1}{2}$–1in)
Height of side-wall line (the diagonal line joining the front-wall line and the back-wall line)

The service boxes shall be entirely enclosed on three sides within the court by lines, the short line forming the side nearest to the front wall, the side wall bounding the fourth side.

The internal dimensions of the service boxes shall be 1.60m (5ft 3in).

All dimensions in the court shall be measured, where practicable, from the junction of the floor and front wall, at a height of 1m (3ft 3in) above the finished floor.

All lines of the court shall be 50mm (2in) in width and all lines shall be coloured red. In respect of the outer boundary lines on the walls, it is suggested that the plaster should be so shaped as to produce a concave channel along such lines.

Appendix III   **Specification of a racket**

1. Dimensions
(a) Maximum length 685mm (27in)
(b) *Internal stringing*
Maximum length 215mm (8.5in)
Maximum breadth 184mm (7.25in)
(c) *Framework of head*
Maximum width across the face 14mm (0.56in)
Minimum width across the face 9mm (0.36in)
Maximum depth across the face 20mm (0.81in)
Minimum depth across the face 12mm (0.47in)
(d) *Shaft*
Minimum thickness 9mm (0.36in)
(e) Maximum weight (including stringing and bumper strip) 255g (9oz)

2. Construction
At all times, the head or shaft shall not contain edges with a radius of curvature less than 2mm ($\frac{1}{12}$in). Strings and string ends must be recessed within the racket head or, in cases where such recessing is impractical because of the racket material or design, must be protected by a non-marking and securely attached bumper strip made of a flexible material which cannot crease into sharp edges following abrasive contact with floors or walls.

Strings shall be gut, nylon or a substitute material, providing metal is not used. Only two layers of string shall be allowed and these shall be alternately interlaced to form an orthogonal array.

Note to referees on degradation
Rackets which have suffered damage so as to cause a potential hazard must not be used for play, unless the damaged region is repaired adhesively or by wound overlays, such that the damaged region becomes stronger than the material on either side of the damaged zone and has a smooth surface.

Specification for squash-racket balls

The ball must conform to the following:
1. It must weigh not less than 23.3g and not more than 24.6g (approximately 360–380 grains).
2. Its diameter must be not less than 39.5mm and not more than 41.5mm (approximately 1.56–1.63in).
3. It must have a surface finish which guarantees continuing correct rebound.
4. It must be of type specifically approved for championship play by the ISRF.
5. Compression specification:
(i) The ball is mounted in an apparatus and a load of 0.5kg (1.1lb) is applied which deforms the ball slightly. Subsequent deformation in the test is measured from this datum.
(ii) An additional load of 2.4kg (5.28lb) is applied and this deforms the ball further. The deformation from the datum position is recorded.
(iii) The deformation obtained in (ii) should be between 3 and 7mm ($\frac{1}{8}$ and $\frac{1}{4}$in) for balls of playing properties acceptable to the ISRF.

Colour of players' clothing

Organizers may specify regulations concerning players' clothing (including footwear) which must be complied with in their particular tournament or tournaments.
SRA Note. For all events under the control of the SRA, players are required to wear white and/or light matching pastel clothing during the course of play. A coloured trim with a maximum width of 50mm (2in) is permissible. Shoes should be predominently white with only 20 per cent of colour trim inclusive of sole, which must be non-marking. The maximum area for advertising is 50 sq mm (2 sq in). Members countries of the ISRF have a limited discretion to allow advertising of a greater size to be worn for any other events under their control. The referee's decision on compliance shall be final.

Code of conduct

6.1 The following offences may be subject to penalties under Rule 17 and/or disciplinary action:

6.1.1 A player who verbally or physically abuses his opponent, the marker, referee, officials, spectators or the sponsors.

6.1.2 A player who shows dissent to the marker, referee or officials, including foul or profane language and obscene or offensive gestures.

6.1.3 A player who abuses playing equipment or the court.

6.1.4 A player who fails to comply with the conditions of entry of a tournament including any rules with regard to clothing or advertising.

6.1.5 A player who having entered a tournament or accepted an invitation to play withdraws from the event or fails to attend.

6.1.6 A player who fails to complete a match.

6.1.7 A player who defaults from a tournament or event. The disciplinary committee may require evidence or proof of 'bona fide' injury, illness or other emergency situation.

6.1.8 A player who fails to make himself available to meet reasonable requests for interviews by the media.

6.1.9 A player who does not comply with the rules of *spirit of the game*.

Index

Page numbers in *italic* refer to illustrations

adductor stretching, 118
abdominal stretching, 120
aerobic training, 89, 94, 96-8
agility, 90
Alauddin, Gogi, 32
anaerobic training, 89, 94, 99-100
angles, 25-32
    boast, 25-31
appeals, rules, 143-5
arms, circuit training, 109-10
Awad, Gamal, 56
Ayton, Philip, 79

back, circuit training, 108-9
back-wall boasts, 30-1
backhand volley, 24-5
bags, 78
ball
    masking, 57
    rules, 147-8, 158
Barrington, Jonah, 16, 20, 46, 53, 59, 67, 75, 80, 95, 121, 122-3, 132
blood circulation, 86-7, 89
boasts, 25-31, 72-3
    angle, 31
    back-wall, 30-1
    practice, 125-6
    reverse angle, 31-2
    skid, 30-1
    trickle, 31
    volley, 29-30
Borg, Bjorn, 135, 136
Brearley, Mike, 137
breathing, 85-6

calf stretching, 115-16
cardio-respiratory fitness, 88
Cawley, Evonne, 135
circuit training, 98-9, 105-10
clothing, 78, 80
    colour, 157

Colburn, Alan, 121
cold courts, 76
concentration, 135-6
condensation, on courts, 77
condition games, 129-31
conduct
    code of, 158
    rules of, 150
continuity of play, 148-50
cooling, body, 88
corkscrew service, 20-1
courts
    condensation, 77
    dimensions, 155
    movement about, 51-5
    warmth, 76-7
cross-court drives, practice, 124
cross-court drops, 38-40
cross-court lobs, 33-4
cut drop, 40-3
cycling, 97

deception, 56-8
defensive game, 64-6
diary, training, 75, 93
diet, 80-2, 90-2
dimensions
    balls, 157
    courts, 155
    rackets, 156
Dittmar, Chris, *69*
driven service, 20
drives, 12-15
    practice, 123-4
drop volley, 44-8
drops, 34-48
    cross-court, 38-40
    cut, 40-3
    floated, 40
    practice, 127-8
    straight, 35-7

variations, 40-4

eating, 80-2, 90-2
explosive speed training, 99
eyes, injuries to, 79

fat, body, 90
first aid kit, 78
fitness training, 85-120
flexibility, 90
floated drop, 40
food, 80-2, 90-2
footwork
    backhand volleys, 24
    court movement, 53-4
    forehand volleys, 23-4
    straight drops, 35
    swing and, 12, 14-15
forearm stretching, 119-20
forehand volley, 23-4

Gallwey, Tim, 137-8
ghosting, 53-6
Gilks, Gillian, 134
glasses, 79-80
grip, 11-12
ground-stroke kill, 48-9

hamstring stretching, 116-17
hard-hit service, 20
head position, swing and, 15
heart, 86-7
Hickox, Jamie, 31
hip-flexor stretching, 118-19
Hunt, Geoff, 27, 59, 67, 75, 132, *133*

injuries, 78-9
    first aid kit, 78
    pain, 78-9
interference, rules, 145-6
interval training, 100

Jahan, Hiddy, 50, 56, 57

Khan, Jahangir, 24, 43, 46, 51, 55, 64, 67, 122, 132, 141
Khan, Jansher, 63, 83
kill, 48–50
  ground-stroke, 48–9
  practice, 128
  volley, 49–50
knock-up, 82–5

left-handed players, 68
legs, circuit training, 105–7
length, 59–60
lets, rules, 142, 146–7
lifting, posture, 111
lobs, 32–4
  cross-court, 33–4
  practice, 126–7
  service, 19–20
  straight, 32–3
lungs, 85–6
lying, posture, 111

markers, duties of, 151
Martin, Rodney, 60
masking the ball, 57
matches
  hour before, 80–2
  knock-up, 82–6
  mental preparation, 132–8
  preparations for, 75–80
meals, 80–2, 90–2
mental approach, 132–8
mobilizing exercises, 113, 114
movement, about the court, 51–5
muscles, 87
  endurance, 88–9
  endurance training, 101

Norman, Ross, 58, 81
nutrition, 90–2

pace, variation of, 66–7
pain, 78–9
patience, 68–9
Patmore, Angela, 137
planning training, 92–6
posture, 110–11
practice, 121–31
pulse warmers, 113, 114–15

quadriceps stretching, 116

rackets, 78
  grip, 11–12
  specifications, 156
  towelling grips, 78
referees, duties of, 151–2
return of service, 21–3
rules, 139–58
running, 96–7

safety, training, 111–12
Safwat, Ahmed, 29
service, 16–21
  corkscrew, 20–1
  driven, 20
  hard-hit, 20
  lob, 19–20
  practice, 124–5
  return of, 21–3
  rules, 139–40
short volleys, practice, 128–9
shoulder stretching, 119
sitting, posture, 110–11
skid boasts, 30–1
skipping, 97
speed, 89
  explosive speed training, 99
  training, 55
squash bag, 78
standing posture, 110
straight drop, 35–7
strategy, 61–4
strength, 89–90
  training, 102–4
strengths, playing, 67–73
stretching, 76, 94
  exercises, 112–13, 114, 115–20
stroke technique, 11–50
  angles, 25–32
  boasts, 72–3
  drives, 12–15
  kill, 48–50
  lob, 32–4
  rules, 142
  service, 16–21
  volley, 23–5
sweat, 80
swimming, 97–8

swing, 12–15

'T', control of, 60–1
tactics
  control of the 'T', 60–2
  court movement, 51–5
  deception, 56–8
  defensive game, 64–5
  developing the game, 58–73
  pace variation, 66–7
  strategy, 61–4
  strengths, 67–73
  weaknesses, 67–73
tournaments
  mental preparation, 132–8
  physical preparation, 75–80
training, 85–120
  diary, 75, 93
  diet, 90–2
  ghosting, 53–6
  planning, 92–6
  safety, 111–12
  tournament preparation, 75–80
  types, 88–90
trickle boast, 31
trunk stretching, 120

volley boast, 29–30
volley kill, 49–50
volleys, 23–5
  backhand, 24–5
  drop, 44–8
  forehand, 23–4
  practice, 125, 128–9

warm courts, 76–7
warm up, 80, 112–15
  rules, 148
warming down, 80, 115
weaknesses, 67–73
weight, 84
weight training, 101–2
Williams, Dean, 56
wrists
  deception with, 57
  swing, 12
  volleying, 24–5

Zaman, Qamar, 41, 43, 56, 57, 62